On the Mark
And
Half a Bubble *off - Plumb*
Thoughts, Quotes, Observations and Reminiscences of the
<u>Primal Prince</u>
An eclectic forward-looking retrospective

Creative Expressions For Any Occasion And Some That Don't Yet Exist

Peter Pjecha Jr.

ISBN: 9781698684499

Introduction

The quotes of the Primal Prince, i.e., On the Mark and Half a Bubble off Plumb, is a work of both fiction and reality that has been in progress for nearly two decades and spans the gamut of creative, challenging and entertaining thought—thoughts that've been gleaned from a myriad of inspirations; national, social, political, relational, religious etc., and all smelted in the mind of the author and extruded in the manifold creative forms set before the reader. Through these quotes, the author attempts to entertain, enlighten, challenge and stimulate the intellect, emotions and spirit of the reader, as well as regularly tripping their sense of humor by the infusion of the oft ludicrous, comically imbedded quotes they encounter. To be sure, On the Mark will prove to be like no other book of quotes the reader has ever read, and they'll come to find, an education that they'll be glad they didn't miss, and couldn't've done without.

"THERE ARE NO PICKS TO THE KINGDOM OF
HEAVEN, ONLY KEYS."

"HEY PAL, IF I WANTED A MAID,
I'D HAVE GOTTEN MARRIED …
OH-OH—DID I SAY THAT OUT LOUD?"

"DON'T GO KILLING THE MESSENGER NOW, OR
TAKE THIS THING THE WRONG WAY, BUT I'VE
NOTICED THAT AFTER SEEING "THAT" PLASTIC
SURGEON, YOUR WIFE HAS A FACE SCULPTED LIKE
A PICASSO—THAT IS TO SAY …
A RANSOM NOTE."

"DON'T INTERRUPT ME, BECAUSE I'M IN THE
MIDDLE OF A LONG STORY AND A GOOD ONE TOO …
MY LIFE."

"A HANDGUN IS TOO GRAVE AND PERMANENT A
SOLUTION TO A TEMPORARY THOUGH IMMEDIATE
PROBLEM, AS WELL AS BEING TOO TEMPORARY A
SOLUTION FOR A GRINDINGLY CHRONIC PROBLEM."

"EASE AND AN OVERABUNDANCE OF OPTIONS ARE
THE MAKINGS FOR A DISSATISFIED LIFE; HARDSHIP
AND WANT REINFORCE THE BOND OF INTIMACY,
COMMITMENT AND COMMUNITY."

"AMERICAN FOLDING CURRENCY HAS ENOUGH
COTTON RAG IN IT TO BE …
'THE FABRIC OF OUR LIVES.'"

"ORDER ORCHESTRATES CHAOS;
CHAOS CANNOT BRING ORDER INTO BEING."

"A MAN CAN ACQUIRE A TASTE FOR MANY THINGS,
EVEN IF HE HAS NO TASTE."

"AS SOON AS YOU'RE CONCEIVED ETERNITY'S
BEGUN —AND WHEN YOU DIE,
IT CONTINUES WITH YOU."

"WHEN YOU'RE TRAPPED BY A HUNGRY GRIZZLY
OR SURROUNDED BY A PACK OF HUNDRED-AND
FIFTY-POUND HYENAS, DON'T TRY TO RUN AWAY,
BUT FALL DOWN, CURL-UP INTO A TIGHT BALL AND
PRETEND YOU'RE NOT A RICH FOOD SOURCE."

"TEXTING IS A DISTANT RELATIVE AND A
SUBSPECIES OF COMMUNICATION; A LIFE REDUCED
TO THE SHALLOW END OF THE POOL; BEREFT OF
THE MIGHTY RIVERS FLOWING, THE LAKES AND
VAST OCEANS DEEP."

"IF I MUST BE ATTACKED;
I'D RATHER IT BE BY A WAILING WHORE THAN A
WHORING WHALE."

"IF YOU GIVE A MAN A FISH HE'LL EAT FOR A DAY;
IF YOU FEED HIM LOBSTER EVERY DAY,
<u>HE'LL NEVER FISH A DAY IN HIS LIFE.</u>"

"THE ONLY JUSTIFICATION FOR RISKING YOUR LIFE
IS TO PRESERVE IT, OR THAT OF OTHERS."

"BAD CHOICES SOMETIMES LEAD US TO PLACES
WHERE WE CAN NO LONGER CHOOSE THE GOOD."

"I DON'T OFTEN QUOTE MYSELF
BECAUSE MY MEMORY ISN'T AS GOOD AS MY
IMAGINATION."

"HUMAN BEINGS HAVE ALWAYS BEEN FRAGILE
WITH A TENUOUS HOLD ON LIFE INDIVIDUALLY;
NOW FOR THE FIRST TIME IN HISTORY, HUMANITY IS
IN GRAVE PERIL COLLECTIVELY."

"ANGER AND SORROW ARE EMOTIONS GOD CAN
WORK WITH; SELF-PITY AND DEPRECIATION ...
NOT SO MUCH."

"THERE IS NO "WOE IS ME" CLAUSE IN
CHRISTIANITY."

"BREAK INTO MY HOUSE AGAIN
WITH A GUN IN YOUR HAND
—AND MAYBE _NEXT TIME_, I WON'T KILL YA."

"THE FUTURE FOR SOME IS WRITTEN IN STONE,
BUT THE STYLUS IS IN THEIR OWN HAND."

"LEARN TO KEEP YOUR MOUTH SHUT,
BECAUSE NOBODY LIKES A SNITCH—EXCEPT THE
WARDEN."

"YOU NEED AN AUDIENCE TO BE COOL,
BECAUSE NOBODY CAN BE COOL IN A VACUUM,
UNLESS OF COURSE, IT'S IN DEEP SPACE, WHICH
INCIDENTALLY IS MINUS -454.81° FAHRENHEIT TO
BE EXACT."

"I believe numbers have meaning and
significance, but words have power."

"Keep it simple for the simple masses."

"Women by nature are curious,
and men are by nature curious about
women."

"We deserve the monsters we create,
and they own us."

"Heads-up Social Engineers
and Lords of War in the United States;
the wealth, treasure and sustenance of
America is now in the deep pockets of our
enemies right next to our I.O.U.'s
—and any nation who makes weapons for,
or <u>borrows it's way into slavery</u> to it's
enemies, is no longer fit or free,
nor long for this earth."

"You should learn from the devil's
mistakes, but not his successes."

"If you're going to be a namedropper when
you get stopped for speeding by a
Pennsylvania State Trooper, be sure the
name you drop isn't the name of the
guy he caught sleeping with his wife."

"Those who rob others of their
Dignity and human rights,
rob themselves of their humanity."

"If God were to not intervene and stop it, the next global war would be the first war without an aftermath for humanity."

"No, I'm not nuts;
I'm just often caught verbalizing my internal dialogue."

"Just because you've grown accustomed to it doesn't mean it's not bullshit."

"You can't be creatively productive and artistic if you daily exhaust all your mental horsepower employed in drudgery and the mind-numbing minutiae of the mundane."

"In America we haven't quite yet given the monkeys the keys to the zoo, but we're working on giving the chimps the keys to the monkey cages."

"The West we know will never cease until we meet the East."

"The horrors man has had to endure, and the atrocities humanity has witnessed—and all of it at our own hand."

"There but for the grace of God go I—and there despite the grace of God goeth he."

"Most times it won't work unless <u>everyone</u> drinks the Kool-Aid."

"Some were born to lead; some to follow—
and others ...
to stay the hell out of their way."

"Sometimes there are advantages to chaos,
if it's well managed."

"We Americans don't have freedom; we have
the illusion of freedom; which incidentally
pretty much feels the same,
until you test it."

"For more and more people every day, it
isn't sleight of hand that deceives them,
but slight of mind."

"The ones who control the situation,
are the ones who control themselves."

"Some things in this life are as inextricable
as water poured into water."

"The Nazis like all tyrants rose to power
not because of human prowess and
intellect, but because of human weakness."

"The only bus that doesn't leave without
you is the one you're on."

"Everybody dies with a to-do list—
and #1 at the top of everyone's list is ...
"Stay alive!"

"DON'T WAIT FOR IT,
BECAUSE THE DEVIL WILL NEVER GIVE YOU
ENOUGH PREP TIME."

"WE CAN'T TAKE WHAT WE CAN'T TOW, BUT LET'S
NOT DESTROY IT, LET'S LEAVE IT FOR THE NEXT
GUY, BECAUSE ULTIMATELY, WE'LL ALL BE
LEAVING IT FOR THE NEXT GUY ANYWAYS."

"I KNOW THAT HUMANITY ISN'T RIGHT, BECAUSE
LIFE HERE IS JUST ONE BIG CONTINUOUS REPAIR
JOB THAT NEEDS TO BE DONE YESTERDAY."

"DUDE, YOU SAID I'M IGNORANT
WITH A CAPITAL "E,"
WELL I COULDN'T'VE SAID IT BETTER."

"SOME PEOPLE TRY TO CON YOU INTO THINKING
THEY'RE ECCENTRIC, DEEP AND COMPLEX,
WHEN IN REALITY, THEY'RE JUST OBTUSE,
TROUBLED AND CONFUSED."

"YOU CAN'T IGNORE OR PARTNER WITH EVIL,
NOR NEGOTIATE WITH IT; IT MUST BE DESTROYED
WITH EXTREME PREJUDICE AND MALICE OF
FORETHOUGHT."

"IF WE FORGET IT,
THE PAST WILL ALWAYS RETURN
AS OUR PRESENT."

"HERE IN MORTAL LIFE,
WE'RE ALMOST ALWAYS,
ALMOST DONE."

"STEEL SHARPENS STEEL,
BUT ONLY WHEN IT'S HELD
AT THE PROPER ANGLE."

"I SOMETIMES WRITE JUST TO
HEAR MYSELF WRITE."

"IN WAR, NOTHING IS MORE EXPENDABLE THAN
BULLETS AND HUMANITY."

"EITHER I BADLY MISJUDGED THE SPEAKER'S
MESSAGE, OR THE APPLAUDING AUDIENCE ARE
ALL IDIOTS."

"FAR TOO MANY SO CALLED 'PARENTS' THESE
DAYS ASPIRE TO BE NOTHING MORE
THAN SPERM DONORS AND INCUBATORS—
AND THEIR OFFSPRING HAVE BEEN REDUCED TO
MERE SPAWN; SUSTAINED, NURTURED AND
ABSORBED BY THE VAST IMPERSONAL OCEAN OF
THE GLOBAL COMMUNITY."

"SOMETIMES THEIR HAIR'S CUT STRAIGHT,
BUT THEIR HEAD'S OBTUSE."

"YOU'RE NOT A STONE CASTING BIGOT IF YOU
SIMPLY AGREE WITH GOD'S ASSESSMENT OF WHAT
HE DECLARES SIN TO BE."

"EVEN <u>METAPHORIC WINGS</u> GIVE ONE THE POWER
TO RISE ABOVE IT ALL."

"I WOULD PREFER TO HAVE AND ENJOY LIBERTY EVEN IF IT'S BEING ABUSED ALL AROUND ME, THEN TO BE DENIED IT AND HAVE US ALL ENDURE THE ALTERNATIVE."

"SOMETIMES CREATIVITY COMES IN A BARRAGE; OTHER TIMES IT HAS TO BE WRUNG OUT."

"THE TONGUES OF TOO MANY FOLKS MOVE FASTER THAN THEY CAN THINK."

"SOMEONE WHO CAN'T SEE THE GENIUS IN WHAT I'VE BEEN DOING SHOULDN'T BE CRITIQUING IT."

"IN AMERICA WE'RE LIVING IN THE DAYS OF HUSBANDLESS MOTHERS DEFENDING 'CHILDLESS' 'FATHERS' DENYING THEIR FATHERLESS CHILDREN."

"FIGHTING TO DEFEND THE FREEDOM TO SIN WILL ENSURE BONDAGE AND JUDGMENT."

"IT'S EASY TO BE FEARLESS WHEN THERE'S NOTHING TO FEAR."

"MY PHILOSOPHY IS:
IF YOU'VE GOT SOMETHING TO SAY,
PUT IT INTO WORDS."

"THE INTELLECT OF TOO MANY IS THEIR WORST ENEMY; THEIR TONGUE ITS CLOSEST ALLY, AND EVERY TIME THEY OPEN THEIR MOUTH, THEY DEFEAT THEMSELVES."

"Urban survival is often reduced to simply point and shoot —and keep pulling the trigger until you feel safe and your ears stop ringing."

"Bacon, ham, sausage and eggs are not the enemy; the enemies of bacon, ham, sausage and eggs are the enemy."

"America used to win consistently in real life; now we just win in the movies."

"Sometimes the key won't turn because it's not the right key; other times it won't turn because it's not the right lock... there is a difference you know."

"It's not always yours to take just because it's being offered."

"May the best man win, but know this; the best man isn't always the man in the right."

"One's poison must be more potent when one's enemies are more powerful."

"I never regret not having said something... that's why I write."

"The world's off the hook and out of control; our hook, not God's."

"FOR SOME 'THE WORLD IS A GHETTO,'
BECAUSE THEY TAKE THE GHETTO WHEREVER
THEY GO."

"CAN ANYONE TELL ME WHY WE'RE LIVING IN A
WORLD WHERE THINGS ALWAYS VIBRATE LOOSE,
BUT NEVER TIGHTER?"

"THE WORLD NEEDS MORE PRACTICED THINKERS
AND LESS SHOOT FROM THE LIP IGNORANT."

"THE WAY I SEE IT,
AN UNCIRCUMCISED JEW IS A GENTILE;
A CIRCUMCISED GENTILE IS NOT A JEW."

"HAVE YOU EVER NOTICED THAT IT'S THE
NOBODY'S GOING NOWHERE THAT MAKE THE MOST
NOISE GETTING THERE?"

"THE ADVANTAGE OF PRIVACY/SECURITY
FENCING IS THAT NO ONE CAN SEE
WHAT'S HAPPENING ON YOUR SIDE OF THE FENCE;
THE DISADVANTAGE IS, THAT NOBODY CAN SEE
WHAT'S HAPPENING <u>TO YOU</u>,
ON YOUR SIDE OF THE FENCE."

"IF YOU WANT TO BE HAPPY IN LIFE, LEARN TO
ENJOY THE PROCESS AS WELL AS THE PRODUCT."

"ART CAN BECOME GARBAGE IF YOU DON'T KNOW
WHEN TO QUIT MESSING WITH IT."

"MY PHILOSOPHY IS, JUST IGNORE-UM,
UNLESS THEY START SHOOTIN' AT YA;

IN WHICH CASE, GIVE-UM YOUR MOST INTENSE
FOCUS AND UNDIVIDED ATTENTION
AND BLOW-UM-AWAY INTO A RED VELVET MIST."

"AMERICA HAS FALLEN AND IS SO BEREFT OF
RESPECT, REDUCED AND DIMINISHED, THAT WE
DON'T EVEN HAVE INFLUENTIAL CONTROL OVER
OUR ALLIES, LET ALONE POWER OVER OUR
ENEMIES."

"SOMETIMES THE PROPER DIRECTION IS THE
DIRECTION WE CAME FROM."

"THERE ARE SOME PLACES IF YOU GO THERE
IGNORANT, YOU'LL STAY THAT WAY,
AND IF YOU GO THERE SMART AND CREATIVE,
THEY'LL BE SURE TO DUMB YOUR ASS DOWN."

"LIKE MY OLD GRANDDADDY USED TO SAY:
'BOY, IF AT FIRST YOU DON'T SUCCEED,
DO IT AGAIN...BUT THIS TIME DO IT RIGHT.'"

"CLOISTERED, SEQUESTERED AND
ENSCONCED IN IGNORANCE...
SOUND LIKE ANYONE YOU KNOW?"

"I'M NOT A WRITER YET PROLIFIC...
BUT PROFOUND."

"THE DIFFERENCE BETWEEN A SHARP KNIFE
AND A DULL KNIFE IS THAT THE DULL KNIFE
SHOULD BE SHARP."

"I'VE HEARD OF A DUMPSTER FULL OF BUMS,
BUT SOME GIRLS ARE A BUMSTER FULL OF DUMB."

"AMERICA CAN NO LONGER AFFORD
TO BE AMERICA."

"YOU CAN'T ESCAPE YOUR OWN DREAMS,
NOR THE DREAMS OF OTHERS."

"I KNEW THAT; I JUST COULDN'T ACCESS IT."

"IN SOME COLORFUL PRECINCTS,
THEY KNOW HOW TO PUT THE <u>DIS</u>
AND THE <u>FUNK</u> IN DYSFUNCTION."

"THERE'S NOTHING WRONG WITH ALTERING YOUR
STATE OF CONSCIOUSNESS UNLESS YOU'RE
ALTERING IT TO A DIMINISHED STATE."

"THERE IS A DAY OF RECKONING AND IT'S
HAPPENING EVERY DAY,
IT'S JUST NOT ALWAYS NOTICED."

"IN A PERFECT WORLD, THINGS DROPPED
WOULDN'T BE CAUGHT BEFORE THEY HIT THE
GROUND AND SHATTERED, THEY WOULDN'T BE
DROPPED IN THE FIRST PLACE."

"MAKE EVERY EFFORT TO CONTROL
YOUR DESIRE TO CONTROL."

"THOSE THAT INVENT THEMSELVES HAVE NO
IDENTITY, BECAUSE THEY'RE MERELY THE
PRODUCT OF THE ONE WHO CREATED THEM."

"I DON'T EVER REMEMBER BEING HANDED
ANYTHING ON A SILVER PLATTER, EXCEPT MAYBE
AT TIMES, MY HEAD."

"HISTORY IS ALWAYS INEVITABLE,
AS WELL AS THE FUTURE."

"IT MAY BE A TALL ORDER,
BUT I WANT TO SUCCEED AT BEING MYSELF."

"I'M GOING TO SEE IF REST CAN ACCOMPLISH
WHAT LABOR COULD NOT."

"I EXHAUST MYSELF TRYING TO
BRING ORDER TO CHAOS
—AND ALL I END UP DOING IS BRINGING
CHAOS TO THE ORDER OF MY LIFE."

"I COULDN'T'VE DONE IT WITHOUT ME."

"SOMETIMES WHEN A KNOT CAN'T BE UNWOUND,
IT NEEDS TO BE CUT ASUNDER OR THROWN INTO
THE FIRE AND BURNED APART."

"THE CURSE OF A WRITER HAS FOREVER BEEN...
I COULD'VE SAID IT BETTER."

"I WANT TO BE A HERO ON THE SIDE THAT WINS;
I DON'T CARE TO BE A HERO IN A LOST WAR."

"SEEING AS WE'RE CHILDREN OF THE KING;
IT WOULDN'T DO TO BE ANYTHING BUT NOBLE."

"WHEN THE NEWS CHANGES I'LL START
LISTENING TO IT AGAIN."

"I'M QUITE CERTAIN THAT HEAVEN WILL BE IN
ULTRA HIGH DEF."

"BEING GIVEN LADY GAGA AS A WIFE IN PARADISE
IS THE ISIS TERRORIST'S WORST NIGHTMARE;
ESPECIALLY IF THE MEAT DRESS SHE HAPPENS TO
BE WEARING AT THE TIME IS MADE OUT OF THINLY-
SLICED PROSCIUTTO."

"MY LIFE EXPECTANCY IS TO LIVE AS LONG
AS GOD WANTS ME TO."

"WHAT DO I THINK YOU ASK?
I THINK I'D LIKE TO STICK AROUND LONG ENOUGH
TO SEE HOW THIS THING ENDS
AND THE NEW THING BEGINS."

"THE WRATH OF MAN IS BUT FOR A RELATIVE MERE
MOMENT; THE WRATH OF GOD IS ETERNAL."

"I'VE BEEN THE MAN I'VE BEEN LONG ENOUGH."

"Words like guns can be tools, weapons,
or tragedy waiting to happen."

"I don't know if I should be sad about it
or glad, but the only bad influence
in my life is me."

"Because I'm a purist,
the only thing I put in my coffee are my lips."

"You'll have to pardon my scrawl,
but it's always been chicken scratch."

"If doing what's right doesn't work
then nothing will."

"Make every effort <u>not</u> to make the food
you eat <u>the enemy</u>, because if you do,
it will be."

"Offence taken is just life reminding you...
you ain't all that."

"When you cook the books,
they're all geniuses."

"The best advice you can give a kid is...
'You've got to hold it together long enough
to get your head screwed on straight.'"

"I DON'T MIND GOING TO THE HIBACHI
RESTAURANTS AS LONG AS I DON'T HAVE TO
CATCH GRILLED SHRIMP WITH MY FACE."

"EVERYONE WANTS TO BE SOMEBODY UNIQUE,
AND ALL THE MIMICS END UP BEING...
IS EACH OTHER."

"I DON'T THANK THE ANIMAL I EAT FOR GIVING ITS
LIFE; I THANK THE LORD GOD OF HEAVEN AND
EARTH FOR GIVING ME THE ANIMAL TO EAT."
"ON THE CUSP IS <u>NO MAN'S</u> LAND."

"DON'T MAKE THE OFT REPEATED MISTAKE
OF BELIEVING THAT A HANDOUT IS A HAND-UP,
FOR WHEN YOU EXTEND YOUR SAVING HAND TO
SOMEONE, IT HAS TO BE EMPTY FOR THEM TO
GRASP IT."

"DEPENDING ON HOW ONE CHOOSES IN THIS LIFE,
PHYSICAL DEATH IS NOT THE END OF JOY,
NOR IS IT THE END OF SUFFERING...
BUT THE FULFILLMENT OF IT."

"WHEN IT COMES TO MORAL INSANITY AS OPPOSED
TO TRUE MENTAL INSANITY, IT'S NOT THAT THE
FORMER CAN'T BE CHOSEN AGAINST, IT'S THAT
THE "AFFLICTED," CHOOSE NOT TO CHOOSE
AGAINST IT."

"THERE YET EXISTS THE HOPEFUL MYTH THAT
WHAT ONE SOWS, ONE SHALL NOT ALSO REAP."

"There is no ugliness more grievous than that made of beauty, nor fairer beauty than that turned from ugliness."

"It's not a contradiction for me to be able to hold two opposing thoughts in my head at the same time, to be applied at different occasions of course."

"The private sector, business and industry are the wheels that grind and the engines that produce; federal, state and local government are but the grease that lubricates the machinery, and if the facilitating grease is withheld; the former will eventually find a creative and more accommodating replacement for the latter."

"I've found that being generous doesn't make you poor."

"One of the niceties of having a cell phone is...you don't have to answer it."

"Sadly, it's not always 'monkey-see monkey-do;' sometimes it's 'monkey-see monkey-do 'monkey-die.'"

"Worthy of the same grace You extend to me is the grace You extend to all, therefore, no one is beneath me, for beneath me are the Everlasting Arms that hold ALL OF US, of equal value, on the same plane."

"Regarding the global Moslem jihad; we're
already fighting World War III,
though in slow motion and subject to
escalation...America's at war all right, we
just don't know to what degree."

"One 'cockroach' killing another
is a win-win situation for all of us
non-cockroaches."

"I don't mind folks pickin' my brain;
as long as they take what they need
and leave the rest."

"Fat, our friend, is good,
especially when it's covered with salt."

"I don't want my clothes or choice of car to
say anything about me except...
'He's not a bum.'"

"America was once a great idea,
but we've run out of investors."

"If you keep filling the trough, the 'pigs'
will keep going there and eating;
if you stop filling the trough, they'll go out
and start rooting."

"The only one that needs to know I'm not
going to be in to work in the morning
is the guy replacing me."

"Always save your sales receipt from the Bodega, just in case you have to return a malfunctioning rotisserie chicken."

"When it comes to buying gold and silver as a hedge against inflation and the collapse of the U.S. dollar, the only question I have to ask is—'What's the best and most secure container according to current Consumer Reports for burying it all in my back yard—a coffee can, or mason jars?'"

"Time flies when you're sleeping."

"In this life one man's mistake is another man's mainstay."

"Because he knows his time is short, Satan is no longer clever and surreptitious when he attacks—and even if you're a casual observer, you can see his fingerprints all over the global crime scene."

"It's not easy not being the man I want to be."

"Some folks, they're so full of shit they need sideboards."

"I feel America's catching a wayward breeze and tacking towards the abyss."

"LIKE MY OLD GRANDDADDY USED TO SAY:
'BOY, IF YOU'RE FIXIN' ON BEIN' A FEAR MONGER,
DON'T GO MARRYING A HYPOCHONDRIAC
WOMAN.'"

"UNREGENERATE HUMANITY HAS A PERNICIOUS
AUTOIMMUNE DISEASE FROM WHICH IT CANNOT
HEAL, BUT ONLY DESTROYS ITSELF."

"BESMIRCH MY GOOD NAME,
AND I'LL BE ALL-OVER-YOU LIKE A MEAT DRESS
ON LADY GAGA."

"I NEVER READ THE OBITUARIES BECAUSE
I'M NOT THAT MORBIDLY CURIOUS ABOUT THOSE
WHO'VE DIED; I'M MORE INTERESTED IN WHO'S
STILL ALIVE."

"PEOPLE ARE WILLING AT TIMES TO SAY THEY'RE
SORRY, BUT THEY'RE NOT TOO OFTEN INCLINED TO
SAY ... 'I WAS WRONG.'"

"HE THAT WAITS FOR THE SUN TO RISE WILL NOT
BE DISAPPOINTED; HE WHO LONGS FOR THE NIGHT
TO FALL SHALL NOT BE COMFORTED."

"YOU DON'T NEED TO REHEARSE TELLING THE
TRUTH; ONLY LIES NEED PRACTICE."

"IT'S NEVER BEEN SAID BECAUSE IT'S NEVER
NEEDED TO BE SAID; UNTIL JUST NOW."

"THE ONLY THING BOTH BARRING AND BRIDGING
MAN'S WAY TO THE CROWN...IS THE CROSS."

"IN A WORLD OF AMBIGUITY AS TO WHAT IS GOOD
AND EVIL; GOOD IS THE MAN I'M STRIVING TO BE;
EVIL IS THE MAN THAT'S TRYING TO STOP ME
—AND WE'RE OFTEN THE SAME MAN."

"UNTIL KINGDOM COME,
A SWEATBAND WILL BE MORTAL MAN'S
EARTHLY CROWN."

"SOMETIMES THE DETAILS IN THE EXPLANATION
ARE MORE PAINFUL THAN NOT KNOWING AT ALL."

"IN MY EXPERIENCE,
LIFE WON'T LET YOU DO ONE THING AT A TIME."

"I'M AFRAID THAT WHEN THOSE DOING TRIAGE
SEE ORGAN DONOR ON THE LICENSE, THE
EFFORTS OF THE HERO'S MAY SUBCONSCIOUSLY
MITIGATE, BECOME PRACTICAL AND ERR ON THE
SIDE OF ORGANS."

"NOT ALL THINGS ARE EQUAL;
IF YOU SHAVE WITH THE SAME RECKLESS
ABANDON WITH WHICH YOU WIPE YOUR ASS…
IT'S GOING TO SHOW."

"CALIFORNIA IS A STATE THAT HAS MANY GREAT
EXPECTATIONS AND MAINTAINS VERY HIGH
STANDARDS…EXCEPT FOR ITS PEOPLE."

"QUIT FUSSING ABOUT IT AND JUST DRINK IT;
WATER'S WATER, AND IT'S MORE SIMILAR THAN IT
IS DIFFERENT."

"DON'T BE TOO BUSTED-UP ABOUT IT;
EVERYONE GETS THEIR TURN AT BEING THE
FLY IN THE OINTMENT, OR THE TURD IN THE
PUNCHBOWL."

"NO MATTER WHAT THEY MIGHT SAY, DEFENDING
THE INNOCENT DOESN'T MAKE YOU GUILTY, BUT
DEFENDING THE GUILTY NEGATES YOUR
INNOCENTS: YES, THE ACCUSED ARE ENTITLED TO
A DEFENSE, BUT ONLY IF ONE BELIEVES THEY'RE
INNOCENT—OR, THEIR DEFENDERS KNOW THEY'RE
GUILTY AND DON'T CARE."

"A MAN IS NEITHER GOOD NOR EVIL
UNLESS AND UNTIL HE PROVES IT."

"'CONGRATULATIONS!
YOU'VE JUST NOW BEEN SELECTED THE LUCKY
WINNER OF A THREE-WEEK ALL-EXPENSE PAID
VACATION TO THE SUNDRENCHED BEACHES OF
THE BRITISH VIRGIN ISLANDS. SIMPLY TEXT OR
CALL THE ENCLOSED TOLL-FREE NUMBER, ENTER
YOUR BANK ACCOUNT/DEBIT AND PIN NUMBERS—
AND WE'LL GET BACK TO YOU!
THANKS,
C.E.O. BRYTON SUNNY'TRAN"

"IF THERE'S SOMETHING YOU CAN DO ABOUT IT BY
ALL MEANS DO SO; IF THERE'S NOTHING YOU CAN
DO ABOUT IT—THEN JUST ROLL WITH IT."

"OH, SHE'S ROUGH ALL RIGHT,
BUT IT'S NOT ALL THE YEARS OF HARD LIVIN' AND
HEAVY DRINKIN' WHICH IS NOW WATER UNDER THE
BRIDGE; IT'S MORE THE BEATING 'SHE'S TAKEN'
'ON THE ROCKS.'"

"WHEN YOU SEE THE POOR AND LESS FORTUNATE
BE COMPASSIONATE AND THANKFUL;
WHEN YOU CONSIDER THOSE BLESSED AND MORE
PROSPEROUS, BE ENCOURAGED AND HOPEFUL."

"AN UNLOADED GUN IS NO SAFER THAN A LOADED
GUN, ESPECIALLY WHEN YOU'RE USING IT FOR
SELF-DEFENSE."

"FORGET ABOUT REALITY—EVEN IN MY DREAMS
AND FANTASIES I DON'T END-UP WITH THE GIRL
AND LIVING HAPPILY EVER AFTER."

"WHAT DO I THINK?...
I THINK THE WORLD'S F.U.B.A.R."

"THE TERRORISTS OF ISIS AND THEIR ILK DO WHAT
THEY WILL BECAUSE THEY HAVE NO MORAL OR
SOCIAL CONTRACT WITH CIVILIZED HUMANITY."

"A GOOD WRITER DOESN'T USE MORE WORDS OR
LESS WORDS, HE USES THE RIGHT WORDS—
AND IN THE RIGHT ORDER—AND EXPRESSED AT THE
RIGHT TIME."

"I DON'T WANT A WOMAN IN MY LIFE THAT WOULD
MAKE ME EXCLUSIVELY HER OWN,
BUT ONE WHO WOULD MAKE ME <u>WANT TO BE</u>,
EXCLUSIVELY HERS."

"I LOVE MY JOB; IT'S MORE FUN THAN A BARREL OF
BLOOD-SUCKING AND TWEAKING
METH-HEADED RAZOR-TOOTHED BABY MONKEYS."

"NONE OF WE CHRISTIANS OUGHT TO EVER LET
OURSELVES BECOME ANY OF SATAN'S
"LEGITIMATE" BUSINESS."
("SATAN, I'M NONE OF YOUR BUSINESS.")

"OH, YOU'LL KNOW IT'S TIME TO GO WHEN YOU
START TO FEEL LIKE THE TOOL THEY USE TO
SCRAPE THE CRAP OFF THEIR SHOES."

"TOO MANY PEOPLE THESE DAYS ARE A SELF-
FULFILLING PROPHECY BEING PLAYED-OUT IN REAL
TIME AND TO ROUSING ANTI-ACCLAIM."

"IT DOESN'T MATTER HOW EASY IT IS,
IF IT'S NOT IMPORTANT TO YOU,
YOU'RE PROBABLY NOT GOING TO DO IT."

"BREAK THE CYCLE OF VICTIMHOOD;
IF YOU'RE CLAIMING TO BE A VICTIM, YOU'RE
CLAIMING TO BE WEAK—
AND WEAKNESS IS PROVOCATIVE—AND WHAT IT
PROVOKES, IS MORE VICTIMIZATION."

"DON'T PURSUE ANY GREAT OR HEROIC
ENDEAVORS WHILE UNDER THE INFLUENCE,
BECAUSE YOU'LL PROBABLY FAIL—
AND IF YOU SUCCEED, YOU MAY NOT REMEMBER
WHAT YOU'VE DONE OR HOW YOU'VE DONE IT."

"IF YOU SEE EVERYTHING AS AN OPPORTUNITY
INCLUDING ADVERSITY, YOU'LL SUCCEED."

"I'D RATHER SEE A STRONG WOMAN IN A POSITION
OF POWER AND AUTHORITY THAN A WEAK MAN."

"It's very telling that as per the Koran,
Mohammed had no good use and nothing
good to say about the— 'stay at home'—
i.e., <u>moderate</u> Moslems."

"In humanity there are the mortal,
the immortal—
and the dammed."

"Too many Americans cultivate
and treat their bodies like fat farms
and lard depositories—amply stocked
and fueled by cholesterol, carbs and
salty goo-fat gravy."

"I love being creative—and I've also noticed,
I'd rather be creative than high."

"I expect better of humanity therefore
I demand it!"

"Just because it's chic, ubiquitous and non-
stigmatic doesn't make it right."

"A coward is the biggest threat to any
man's kingdom; especially if he's the king."

"You haven't won anything when you take
something that doesn't belong to you...
you're just a thief.

"You can't persuade anyone by condemning
them; condemnation is not a persuasive
argument."

"Yep, I eat a lot of carbs, but I always
balance it out with fat and sugar."

"Kids these days are learning all kinds of
bad habits with no adults around
who care enough about it to stop them."

"Remember; when you're the lead
interrogating Detective;
Piss first and ask questions later."

"Life is like a walk down
memory lane backwards."

"You can set a man at liberty,
but you can't make him free."

"If you start everyone out at 100%
and they fade or fall into disfavor in your
estimation in this ranking system, make
every effort to bring them back to 100% as
quickly and cleanly as possible, as the onus
is always on you."

"What do you mean, 'No child left behind?'...
Stand-up, be counted and take ownership
y'all— Cus we've got-ta get ourselves a
policy of...'No Baby Daddy left behind!'"

"My friend criticized me and said:
'You think you're smarter than you are.'
And I told him, 'No actually, I think I'm not
as smart as I am.'"

"MOST CREATIVE PEOPLE AREN'T JUST CREATIVE,
THEY'RE <u>AMBITIOUSLY CREATIVE OPPORTUNISTS</u>."

"DON'T BE AN UNDERACHIEVER—
IF LIFE HANDS YOU LEMONS—MAKE CHAMPAGNE."

"I TOLD HIM: 'SHE'S STUNNINGLY BEAUTIFUL,
FABULOUSLY WEALTHY AND SHE'S SINGLE DUDE—
THE ONLY THING IS, SHE LIKES GAY GUYS.'
AND HE SAID…'WELL JUST HOW GAY DO YOU
HAVE TO BE?'"

"MOST PEOPLE LIVE LIVES OF OBLIVION;
THEY DON'T KNOW WHAT'S HAPPENING,
THEY DON'T KNOW WHAT'S HAPPENED,
THEY DON'T KNOW WHAT'S COMING—
AND WHAT'S MORE…THEY DON'T CARE."

"I' THINK I'D MAKE A MUCH BETTER THEORETICAL
ASTROPHYSICIST THAN AN ACTOR,
BECAUSE MY IMAGINATION IS FAR BETTER THAN
MY MEMORY FOR DIALOGUE."

"ONE'S TRADITION MAY BE A VERY INTERESTING
THING, BUT IT DOESN'T ALWAYS TRANSLATE WELL
INTO OTHER CULTURES."

"IF ONE WERE WORTHY OF GRACE, IT WOULD
CEASE TO BE GRACE—AND WE MUST ALLOW GOD
TO EXTEND THE FREE FLOW OF HIS GRACE
THROUGH US, TO OTHERS, WITHOUT
INTERFERENCE OR INTERRUPTION."

"HANNIBAL LECTER?
... YAH, HE HAD ISSUES."

"I USED TO THINK I WAS LIVIN'-THE-DREAM;
HERE COME TO FIND,
I'M JUST DREAMING ABOUT THE LIFE."

"I WRITE IT BECAUSE IT'S TRUE; I'M SAD
THAT IT'S TRUE; I DON'T WANT IT TO BE TRUE,
BUT WE'VE MADE IT TRUE. THE HANDWRITING IS
ON THE WALL; BY DESIGN AND OF NECESSITY
AMERICA IS ON ITS WAY OUT; THE <u>PERFECT STORM</u>
IS COMING FOR US ALL."

"WHEN SUBMITTING AN ACCIDENT REPORT
ALWAYS INCLUDE: I WAS FOLLOWING EVERY
CONCEIVABLE PRECAUTION AND BEING
EXTREMELY CAREFUL WHEN THE ACCIDENT
<u>OCCURRED TO ME</u>."

"I WAS TOLD BY THE UNIVERSE ...
'SHUT-UP!'—AND STOP MAKING NOISE,
UNLESS AND UNTIL YOU'VE GOT THE RIGHT
ANSWER."

"IN HIS DAY, BARAK OBAMA, HIS HANDLERS AND
THE MACHINERY OF HIS CHICANERY CONNED THIS
NATION BECAUSE WE WANTED TO BE CONNED; WE
WERE READY TO BE CONNED; WE NEEDED TO BE
CONNED; WE CHOSE TO BE CONNED—AND
THEREFORE ... DESERVED TO BE CONNED."

"I TOO OFTEN GET FRUSTRATED, ANGRY AND LOSE
CONTROL BEFORE I REALIZE THAT I HAVE
OPTIONS."

"You'll never find the skeletal remains of
God once clothed in human flesh—
for if an immortal chooses to die,
he doesn't cease to be immortal unless he
never lives again—yet somewhere in
Jerusalem, there's an empty tomb that
proves He does."

"One doesn't have to be prolific;
just profound."

"The Moslems seem to need weapons to
follow Islam, but can they practice Islam
without the Kaaba and Mecca?"

"It's hard to see God through
the fog of war."

"I've been using words for a long time to get
my thoughts out there;
now they're using me to be heard."

"Being an American patriot, I believe that
when one is designing a *knife*,
one should always err on the side of more
blade than *handle*."

"Ashes to ashes dust to dust ...
there's too much 'dust' in this world—
yet all must this way come."

"I don't want to be a better man than
others, just a better man than me."

"The game of brinksmanship is the intrepid,
innate or acquired ability, to fill a glass to
the rim—and then continue to add drop by
crowning drop of precious fluid without
causing it to overflow—while your
adversary in his turn doing the same, does."

"Being shot multiple times like the rapper
50-Cent is no badge of honor,
it's more of a badge of—I forgot to duck and
take cover … <u>repeatedly!</u>"

"Know this; one day all the monsters will
go down shrieking in flames of horror."

"If your pillow doesn't work anymore,
there's probably something wrong with
your head."

"If you're going to lose it, trust me, this is
the place to do it; it won't cost you a thing
and it won't even be noticed."

"We Americans are dissatisfied because
we're no longer coming to 'the table' as a
lean and hungry nation; now the lean and
hungry peoples of the world are coming
strong and <u>uninvited</u> to sit down at <u>our</u>
table and sup with us."

"Alcohol like fire one must respect,
control and use prudently,
or use it <u>not at all</u>."

"I'VE NOTICED THAT WHEN THE "ELECTRICIANS"
COME TO WHERE I WORK, THINGS EVERYWHERE
START LOOKING BRIGHTER—AND WHEN THE COPS
SHOW-UP—ALL MY COWORKERS ARE WEARING
SUNGLASSES."

"I WAS TALKING TO MY NEPHEW AND HAPPENED
TO MENTION THAT MY T.V. WAS DOWN FOR TWO
DAYS BECAUSE THERE WAS ICE AND SNOW ALL
OVER MY DIRECT T.V. DISH. HE ASKED
INCREDULOUSLY: 'WHAT DID YOU DO!' ...
I SAID— 'HAVE YOU EVER HEARD OF A BOOK?'—
TO WHICH HE REPLIED ...
'HOW'D YOU GET THE ICE AND SNOW OFF YOUR
DIRECT T.V. DISH WITH A BOOK?'
[INCIDENTALLY, I NO LONGER HAVE DIRECT T.V.]."

"YOU CAN USE MARIJUANA TO PROMOTE
CREATIVITY IN THE SAME WAY YOU CAN USE
WHISKEY FOR GUTS."

"GOD DIDN'T CALL US TO BE CRITICAL JUDGES,
BUT JUDICIOUS SERVANTS."

"FALLING BACK IS EASY; 'SPRING FORWARD' IS
WHERE THE CHALLENGE LIES;
YET YOU'RE ALWAYS SAFER WHEN YOU *SPRING
FORWARD*, THAN WHEN YOU *FALL BACK*."

"IF MY CURSIVE STANDARD WERE AS BEAUTIFUL
AS MY FONT CHOICE IN TYPING,
I'D ALWAYS USE A FOUNTAIN PEN ...
BUT ONLY IF IT HAD SPELL-CHECK."

"I NEVER DRINK IN BARS;
THEY'RE TOO FULL OF LONELY AND DEPRESSINGLY
SAD PEOPLE TRYING DESPERATELY NOT TO BE."

"REGARDING GOOD CITIZENSHIP AND
GOVERNANCE; I DO MY PART AND THEY DON'T DO
THEIR PART ... AND THAT'S THE SADDEST PART
ABOUT IT ALL."

"ALWAYS CHECK THE CONTRAINDICATIONS:
IF YOUR HEAD SWELLS TO TWO OR THREE TIMES
ITS NORMAL SIZE, DISCONTINUE USE AND SEEK
EMERGENCY MEDICAL HELP IMMEDIATELY."

"NO ONE TAKES TURNS IN HELL;
THE TERMS ARE CONCURRENT AND ETERNAL;
THE SENTENCE ABSOLUTE."

"THE WORLD IS A HARSH PLACE; NEEDS DON'T
HAVE TO BE MET ANY MORE THAN DESIRES."

"DON'T BE WHERE YOU OUGHT NOT TO BE DOING
WHAT YOU OUGHT NOT TO BE DOING AND YOU
WON'T HAVE TO WORRY ABOUT GETTING CAUGHT
OR GOING SPLAT."

"IT SEEMS LIKE A PARADOX THOUGH TRUE, THAT
BECAUSE WE HAVE FREE WILL,
GOD WANTS TO BE IN CONTROL OF US,
IN CONTROL OF OURSELVES."

"OUR TECHNOLOGY IS GETTING MORE COMPLEX
ALLOWING MAN TO BECOME SIMPLER."

"A MOMENT OF WEAKNESS IS STILL JUST A
MOMENT OF CHOICE."

"THE SEX DRIVE OF SOME MAY NOT BE WHAT IT
COULD BE, SHOULD BE, OR THEY'D LIKE IT TO BE,
BECAUSE THEY NO LONGER HAVE A <u>DESIRABLE</u>
DESTINATION TO <u>DRIVE</u> TOWARD."

"GREAT MEN AND WOMEN, DOING GREAT THINGS,
IN A GREAT CAUSE, FOR A GREAT NATION,
THAT THEY LOVE GREATLY ...
SOUND LIKE ANYONE YOU KNOW AMERICA?"

"SOME OF THOSE WHO ARE BASE AND WICKED
COME TO KNOW THAT THEY'RE WICKED
INDIVIDUALLY EVENTUALLY, BUT THEY'LL NEVER
COME TO KNOW IT COLLECTIVELY."

"THE CAFETERIA LADIES IN THE MIDDLE SCHOOL I
WORK AT ARE QUITE PROGRESSIVE AND CUTTING-
EDGE CHIC; ONE NAMED CHIARA EVEN PROMISED
THAT SHE'D MAKE AND WEAR A MEAT DRESS OUT
OF BOLOGNA OR SLICED HAM AS A HOMAGE TO
HER IDOL, LADY GAGA."

"IF IT <u>DOESN'T</u> GRIEVE ME;
I'M A LESSER MAN THAN I THOUGHT."

"NOW THAT I'M THINKING ABOUT IT,
I'D RATHER HAVE MARILYN MONROE WITH MY
GIRLFRIEND'S PICTURE ON <u>HER</u> SHIRT."

"TRY SAYING, 'GOOGLE THE GABOR'S'
(3) TIMES FAST."

"I RARELY DREAM AT NIGHT; I DO ALL MY DREAMING DURING THE DAY—AND INTERESTINGLY ENOUGH, I DON'T REMEMBER ANY OF IT."

"I THINK ONE OF THE THINGS THE LIBRARY OF CONGRESS IS IN DIRE NEED OF IS A COPY OF THE CONSTITUTION TRANSLATED INTO JIVE."

"I CAN SPEAK ENGLISH, SPANISH AND I'M FLUENT IN EMOTICON; IN WHICH BY THE WAY, I'M GOING TO EVENTUALLY WRITE MY MEMOIRS."

"THE GREATEST INJUSTICE OF ALL IS <u>NOTHING</u> BEING DONE ABOUT THE INJUSTICE... <u>BY THOSE WHO CAN</u>."

"THEY TOLD ME, 'JUST KEEP ON MOVING JACKASS UNTIL YOU GET TO NOWHERE,' AND I'M GLAD I <u>DIDN'T</u> TAKE <u>THAT</u> ADVICE FROM <u>THOSE</u> STRANGERS, ESPECIALLY WHEN THEIR DIRECTIONS SEEMED A TAD SKETCHY."

"<u>TRUST ME</u>; WHEN GOD WAGES WAR AGAINST SATAN AND THOSE HE'S DECEIVED AT THE BATTLE OF ARMAGEDDON—IT WILL <u>NOT</u> BE A NAIL-BITER."

"MANY PEOPLE TRULY GOOD, ARE NOT ALL RIGHT."

"CONTRARY TO THE NOTION; HUMANITY <u>IS</u> A WORLD FULL OF PEOPLE WHO REGRET <u>NOT</u> HAVING SAID SOMETHING."

"'Beautiful' ... I love that word ...
especially when it's applied to me and my
creative expressions."

"One always pays a price for becoming
a better man; maturity takes time and
comes dear."

"Record it before you forget it,
or you'll forget it before you record it...
bin there done that."

"It's a good thing I'm not king of the world,
because even I wouldn't be here."

"The way I see it, if we don't get out of here
BEFORE the shit hits the fan,
we'll _be_ the shit that hits the fan."

"You know the smell of summer is in the air
when the waft of skunk is on the breeze."

"Creators create and destroyers destroy—
and sometimes creators create destroyers
that destroy them."

"That on the table, and those at the table
are places of honor;
under the table ... not so much."

"It's not going to end the way you _THINK_ it is,
but by the way God _SAID_ it is."

"Hey, that's just one more thing I forgot
about that I won't have to do now."

"No state is static;
God is looking for those He can trust
with success as well as failure."

"'Hugs are better than drugs is contingent
upon who you're being hugged by ...
or drugged by."

"The world's full of impractical people
doing very impractical things
suffering very practical consequences."

"Trust me dude;
your 'lucky' hat ISN'T the one you were
wearing when you got shot in the head."

"I don't want to touch the ceilings in my life
until I become a far greater man."

"They may not be traditional "hymns" I'm
singing NOW, but in a hundred years they
will be."

"War will never cease because terror and
horror have never stopped man from
waging war."

"It's hard to watch your heroes grow old
and see your enemies becoming younger."

"The only thing God wants us to give
up for Lent is sin."

"Her legions couldn't protect Rome from
itself; there's a lesson to be learned in
that for America."

"He knows he's not the better man and he
refuses to defer to the one who is;
which is why he isn't."

"Much like– 'Extremism in the defense of
Liberty'; 'Extremism in the defense of one's
life 'is no vice.'"

"Seeing as I've got nothing much else
going on in my life, maybe GREATNESS
is the way to go."

"You know you need glasses when you
finally hear: 'Dude ... I don't think those
shiny things are flax seeds from the
multigrain bread I was cuttin'; I think
they're just some kind of brown-shelled
bugs you're eatin'."

"If you were BORN with a ringing in your
ears, you'd never notice it until it stopped."

"It's amazing and stunning to me, the people
that got honorable mention in the Bible."

"IF I'VE BEEN DEEMED WORTHY OF THE GIFT;
IT SEEMS REASONABLE THAT I'D BE DEEMED
WORTHY OF USING IT."

"FOR DOING SOME THINGS,
NOTHING IS A GOOD REASON."

"SOMETIMES A THING MAGNIFIED ONLY EXPOSES
ITS IMPERFECTIONS."

"IT ISN'T THE STEEPNESS OF MOUNTAIN AHEAD
THAT GROUNDS YOU DOWN AND WEARS YOU OUT—
IT'S THE STONE FROM YOUR KIDNEYS PASSING
THROUGH YOUR URETHRA THE JAMS-YOU-UP."

"THE DIFFERENCE BETWEEN A SCROUNGE AND A
BUM IS—IT TAKES EFFORT TO BE A SCROUNGE."

"SOME PEOPLE AREN'T EVEN WORTHY <u>TO</u> SERVE,
LET ALONE <u>BE</u> SERVED."

"I'M MORE A BELT THAN SUSPENDERS KIND OF
GUY, BECAUSE I'D RATHER GIRD MY LOINS THAN
HAVE THEM SUSPENDED."

"HAVE YOU WONDERED LIKE I HAVE, IF THERE WAS
EVER AN AMERICAN INDIAN WHOSE NAME
TRANSLATED INTO ENGLISH WOULD HAVE BEEN—
'*DON'T-GIVE-TWO-SHITS.*'"

"ONE CAN'T CLAIM <u>WOUNDED</u> PRIDE
IF HE HAS NO SHAME."

"YOU <u>CAN'T</u> EDUCATE THE IGNORANCE OUT OF
PEOPLE <u>AGAINST THEIR WILL</u>."

"YOU CAN'T AFFORD TO TRUST ANYONE WHO HAS
NO MANIFEST SENSE OF SELF-PRESERVATION;
IF THEIR LIFE IS CHEAP, HOW VALUABLE TO THEM
CAN YOURS BE."

"IF YOU ASK THE YOUNG PASTOR IN A CHURCH
YOU'RE VISITING—'DO YOU THINK THERE'S HOPE
FOR ME PASTOR?'—AND HE REPLIES,
'HOPE FOR WHAT?' ... YOU MIGHT JUST WANT TO
KEEP ON LOOKING."

"IF YOU'RE FINDING YOU HAVE TO PRETREAT THE
SHIT STAINS IN YOUR SKIVVIES WITH A PAIR OF
SCISSORS, THERE'S A GOOD CHANCE YOU'VE GOT
TOO MUCH FIBER IN YOUR DIET."

"WHAT DOES ONE HAVE TO DO AND HOW FAR
MUST ONE GO, BEFORE IT STOPS BEING '<u>SICK</u>' AND
STARTS BEING DEMONIC?"

"AT TIMES, LIMITS ARE JUST CHALLENGES THAT
ARE MISUNDERSTOOD, NEED TO BE REDEFINED—
AND OVERCOME."

"THE WORLD NOW PAYS BUT A PINCH OF INCENSE
IN LIP SERVICE TO THE GODS THAT ONCE WERE,
WHILE CHRISTIANS WORSHIP IN TRUTH THE LIVING
GOD THAT YET IS."

"CRITICAL MASS" WAS MARIE OSMOND <u>BEFORE</u> NUTRISYSTEM—AND <u>AFTER</u> HER HUSBAND SAID: — 'YIKES!!'"

"THE NAME'S ZDWTNYRFGKMLBPH; ITS LOWER SLOBOVIAN, IT'S SOUNDS JUST LIKE ITS SPELLED AND ROLLS RIGHT OF THE TIP OF YOUR TONGUE— BUT YOU CAN ONLY PRONOUNCE IT IF YOU'RE TRIPPIN' ON L.S.D."

"BE ON GUARD; THOSE TRAPPED BY THE ENEMY, MIGHT STILL BE THE ENEMY."

"WE WERE TOO POOR TO AFFORD MIDDLE NAMES WHEN I WAS A KID; THANK GOD FOR NICKNAMES."

"A GUN MAY NOT BE THE RIGHT ANSWER IF YOU ASK THE WRONG QUESTION."

"I MAY NOT HAVE A VOICE, BUT I DO HAVE A PEN— AND THE ADDRESS OF THOSE WHO HAVE A SWORD AND A FORUM."

"THOSE THAT ARE SPOON-FED THE TRUTH RARELY LEARN TO FEED THEMSELVES."

"SOMETIMES IT'S THE SLINGS, STINGS AND ARROWS; SOMETIMES IT'S THE THORNS AND THISTLES; AND SOMETIMES IT'S THE PINS AND NEEDLES OF OUTRAGEOUS BULLSHIT."

"I've never tried my hand at acting, except
perhaps at times like a jackass; which
indecently … I find I'm really quite good at."

"Invisibility has such a negative
connotation; the invisible man wasn't so
much 'invisible,' as he was visibly
challenged."

"The only thing I'd like to say about the
thugs and drug-fueled gang-bangers in my
neighborhood on the lower east side
throwing lead at each other is—
'I hope they don't miss.'"

"It's a fine line to walk; when you start
identifying with your enemies,
they either become your friends—
or your master."

"You're better off without a gun in your
hand; especially when you've got a drink
in the other one."

"Words have power;
God didn't calculate the world into
existence, He <u>spoke it</u> into being."

"I don't want to live my life just a half-step
ahead of the devil biting my ass."

"Thug-life Rap may not be the direct
<u>cause</u> of thuggery, but it's the <u>effect</u>
that reinforces the cause."

"Exploring the world in comfort is not possible, because most of the world is a very uncomfortable place ... your living room in front of your big screen T.V. ... now <u>that's</u>, a comfortable place!"

"Man is very creative—and many things unheard of are possible, but one has to devolve into prevision and insanity to access them."

"When The Lord my God deals with me on judgment day, I would rather He bring an olive branch to the proceedings than a hickory switch."

"The tag-team of Obama and Kerry surreptitiously negotiating a nuclear deal with the Iranians without verification—was like putting a gun they've never seen before to the head of America, and then pulling the trigger to prove it isn't loaded."

"I don't want to be the puppet of any master; including myself."

"The question is:
'<u>How many angels</u> can dance on the head of a pin?' And my answer is—<u>all of them</u>, if God wants them to—and tell me:
Just how many pins actually <u>need</u> to have angels dancing on their heads anyway?"

"Tell me, is he the guy that got knocked off a kangaroo he was riding by a boomerang ...

CUS IF NOT—THEN I'M THINKIN' OF SOMEBODY
ENTIRELY DIFFERENT."

"SET ASIDE ENOUGH FOR THE PURSES
OF THE POOR—AND YOU'LL ALWAYS HAVE
PLENTY IN YOUR COFFERS."

"OF ALL EARTHLY HORRORS, HUMAN MONSTERS
HAVE ALWAYS BEEN THE WORST KIND."

"SOMETIMES THE BIGGEST 'BALL-AND-CHAIN'
IS THE ONE WEARING IT."

"GOD <u>CURSED</u> THE EARTH INTO A DOG-EAT-DOG
WORLD; IT WAS <u>NEVER</u> HIS INTENT TO—
<u>NOR DID HE</u>, CREATE IT THUS."

"HUMAN HISTORY AND DESTINY IS TO KNOW,
THAT EVEN IF YOU'RE NOT HERE TO LOOK OUT THIS
WINDOW, IT'LL STILL BE A WORLD OF BOTH GOOD
AND EVIL."

"'WE HAVE TO PASS THE BILL SO THAT YOU CAN
FIND-OUT WHAT'S IN IT …' <u>AS PER NANCY PELOSI</u>,
IS TANTAMOUNT TO SAYING: 'FEEL FREE TO STEP
INTO A STEAMING-HOT PILE OF SHIT, BECAUSE
THERE'S ALWAYS A CHANCE YOUR WIFE WON'T
GET PISSED-OFF WHEN SHE NOTICES IT TRACKED
ALL OVER HER BRAND-NEW DINING ROOM
CARPET.'"

"YAH WE'RE STILL IN AMERICA,
BUT JUST BARELY."

"WITH THE UBER-LIBERAL IMMIGRATION
AND WELFARE POLICIES IN THE U.S. OF A.,
THE REST OF THE WORLD IS COMING
HERE TO RETIRE."

"PLAYING THE RACE CARD WAS ONCE THE FINAL
RETREAT AND LAST REFUGE OF A COWARD;
A DESPERATE AND LAZY BEING WHO'D RATHER
TRUST IN THE COLOR OF SKIN FOR ADVANTAGE,
THAN THE CONTENT OF THEIR CHARACTER FOR
JUSTIFICATION; NOW IT'S THE FIRST RESORT AND
MOST PRIMAL KNEEJERK SOCIAL INSTINCT OF THE
SELF-VANQUISHING."

"SOMETIMES TRYING TO STRADDLE THE RUTS IN
YOUR LIFE WILL STEER YOU PRECARIOUSLY CLOSE
TO RUIN AND GOING OVER THE EDGE."

"TOO MANY PEOPLE BURY THEIR FESTERING SIN
UNDER LAYER UPON LAYER OF HEART HARDENING
AND SOUL NUMBING RATIONALIZATION."

"IF YOUR GIRLFRIEND ASKS YOU:
'SAY SOMETHING NICE ABOUT ME BABY, CUS I'M
REALLY FEELIN' KIND-A DOWN TODAY.'
I'D SHY AWAY FROM TELLING HER:
'WELL, YOU'VE GOT GOOD STURDY LEGS AND A
SOLID WALK, YOUR HAIR STYLE AND SHOES ARE
REALLY QUITE SENSIBLE—AND YOU'VE GOT REALLY
BEAUTIFUL SKIN ... 'LOTS IF IT!'"

"IN AMERICA I DON'T WANT THEM TO BE:
'OH, THEY'RE "JUST" WOMEN.' ...
BUT I DO WANT THEM TO BE WOMEN."

"My job doesn't challenge me enough nor
reward me enough—and how could it,
if a far lesser man can could do it
quite handily."

"Fret-not and dread not; God knows who
the wicked are, where they are—
and how to get to them in due time."

"The past is not yet
and the future never was."

"You can become discouraged and offended
by the noble being base, but not by the base
being base ... <u>because they're base</u>!"

"This world is a horrific place,
with oases of diversion,
of which America is the greatest ...
and I'm witnessing it all from the oasis."

"Any state of being but The Divine is a fluid
and temporary condition."

"Charmed lives always come with an
expiration date and a final destination."

"Jesus Christ is my Lord and Savior—and the
weight of an ounce of lead won't change
that. ... Better by far to freely give-up one's
life, than one's Lord and God."

"Do you know what they call half of a dollar bill in America? ... '50 Cent.'"

"Truth like light in the darkness is most in context among lies."

"You have to be able to defy fear before you can defy gravity."

"The quickest way to get <u>even</u> with your enemy is to forgive him."

"If you find an envelope on the ground always examine the contents, because it may contain money ... and hardly ever anthrax."

"All humanity is in some way bound—for in a fallen world, bondage and not liberty is the natural state of things."

"Ignorance is a dish best served by somebody else."

"In Kun Tao Silat Kung Fu, Judo and Aikido, I was taught you can break a person's balance and leverage their weight <u>and or stupidity</u> against them; effortlessly and with devastating results."

"One of our Cafeteria ladies who's also the school's Chef, was relating the curiosity that even though she doesn't drink anything more in the evenings, nor as much

COFFEE DURING THE DAY AT WORK, SHE STILL FINDS HERSELF GOING TO THE BATHROOM MORE FREQUENTLY, TO WHICH I RESPONDED ... 'WELL, MAYBE YOU'RE JUST ABSORBING MORE MOISTURE FROM THE ATMOSPHERE THAN USUAL.'"

"SNIDELY WHIPLASH IS A NAME YOU CAN'T TAKE LIGHTLY OR SAY <u>THREE TIMES</u> QUICKLY."

"WITH WILLIE NELSON IT'S NOT SO MUCH, 'WHISKEY RIVER TAKE MY MIND'—AS SMOKE THROUGH THE RICE PAPER BLOW MY MIND."

"TRUST ME; I'M DOING MORE THAN MY PART TO SAVE THE PLANET, IN FACT, MY CARBON FOOTPRINT IS SO LIGHT THAT BLOODHOUNDS WITH A MASS SPECTROMETER COULDN'T TRACK ME IF I WAS TAKING THEM FOR A WALK."

"I'VE HEARD TELL OF SOME CUTTING-EDGE RENEGADE SURGEONS, HEAVILY FINANCED BY OBSCENELY RICH ENTREPRENEURS WITH DEEP POCKETS, NO CONSCIENCE OR RESERVATIONS, SERIOUSLY CONSIDERING DOING HUMAN HEAD TRANSPLANTS. WELL AND GOOD AND BE THAT AS IT MAY, BUT THE HEAD <u>IS NOT</u> YOUR TYPICAL DONOR ORGAN—AND MY BIG CONCERN IS, WILL THAT INFO BE INDICATED ON MY FUTURE DRIVER'S LICENSE AUTOMATICALLY, OR AM I GOING TO BE ISSUED A SEPARATE AND NEW <u>HEAD DONORS CARD</u> BY THE STATE OF PENNSYLVANIA. D.M.V.

"NEVER REMEMBER TO FORGET SOMETHING AND YOU WILL."

"<u>All</u> failings that impact your life and experiences negatively are <u>moral</u> failings; if not your own, then somebody else's."

"As a Christian, I'm well aware of the fact that I <u>can't</u> surrender <u>without</u> orders— and that <u>those</u> orders … will <u>never</u> come."

"I used to look like that; but it was in my dreams."

"If 'The price of liberty' for America 'is eternal vigilance' then what we're defending is not Liberty but license, which engenders bondage."

"I think I'm going to patent a genetically engineered liquor that when you dilute it with water it gets stronger."

"Saying more doesn't always sweeten the deal and saying less doesn't always close the deal."

"You'll find out 'just what the hell it is', I 'do around here <u>anyway</u>', when I'm not here to do it <u>anymore</u>."

Definition—[Base]
"Having or showing a contemptible mean spirited or selfish lack of human decency. Hey! … I think I know that guy!"

"OH THEY'RE THERE SENATOR—AND THEY'RE STILL
LOOKING, BUT I ASSURE YOU, 'THERE IS NO <u>THERE</u>
THERE'—AND THERE'LL BE NO <u>THERE</u> THERE WHEN
<u>YOU</u> GET THERE, THEREFORE; THE "THERE" <u>YOU'RE</u>
LOOKING FOR ISN'T THERE … AND THERE YOU
HAVE IT SIR, AND THERE IT IS … <u>SO THERE</u>!"

"IT'S NEVER MORE IMPORTANT TO THINK OUTSIDE
THE BOX THAN WHEN YOU'RE IN THE BOX."

"DON'T EVER LET DEFEAT BECOME YOUR DEFAULT
SETTING AND YOU'LL WIN FAR MORE OFTEN THAN
YOU THINK."

"PLATINUM, GOLD, SILVER AND DIAMONDS …
'NAH.' … THE BLOOD OF THE CROSS AT CALVARY
IS THE ONLY CURRENCY AND MEDIUM OF
EXCHANGE THAT MAKES <u>ME</u> FEEL SAFE."

"IN THE LIVES OF SOME,
HATE IS THE LAST THING TO DIE."

"'I KNOW YOU'RE A WOMAN, BUT PLEASE TRY
ACTING LIKE A LADY.' DOESN'T WORK,
UNLESS OF COURSE … SHE IS."

"THE DIFFERENCE BETWEEN A CAREER AND A JOB
IS WHAT KIND OF CAR YOU DRIVE—
AND IF YOU CAN'T SPELL CAREER …
YOU PROBABLY DON'T HAVE ONE."

"'<u>NOT YOU</u>!'—THE PERSON BEHIND YOU'—
IS THE STORY OF MY LIFE."

"Far too many politicians in America these days don't merely have a shit-stain in their skivvies; they've got their tighty whities wrapped around and wedged into a perpetual pile of crap."

"One must consider the fact that:
Far more adversity than we're willing to admit has been overcome by those for whom the bar has been raised and not lowered—for raising the bar doesn't stop those who desire to succeed from doing so, while lowering the bar allows one to <u>proceed</u>, <u>without succeeding</u>."

"The thing that eternal vigilance defends liberty against at great price is hubris and human weakness—and you can't kill that with a gun, it must forever be <u>kept</u> in check and <u>held</u> at bay by the sustained and pure will of the free."

"I perceive people these days are too neurotic and malcontent to live happily <u>at all</u> ... let alone ever after."

"Sometimes you feel the brush of something and think it's nothing—but it's the touch of the devil's hand."

"You may disagree with me, but I believe The Buddha got a lot of practice in time-out as a kid."

"I NEVER TAKE BATHS; ALWAYS SHOWERS,
BECAUSE I LIKE TO WASH THE FILTH CLEAN OFF OF
ME—AND HAVE A PRIMAL FEAR OF STEWING IN MY
OWN RICH JUICES."

"WHEN YOU EXPECT BETTER AND FAR MORE OF
THOSE YOU CLAIM HAVE GREAT POTENTIAL AND A
LOT TO OFFER ... YOU DO THEM NO DISSERVICE."

"BE VERY CAREFUL WITH GUNS AND AROUND
THOSE WHO AREN'T."

"AS WONDERFUL AND INDISPENSABLE AS THEY
ARE; ONE OF THE HARDEST THINGS FOR ROBOTS
TO DO IS WIPE THEIR ASSES WITHOUT TEARING THE
TOILET PAPER."

"COWARDS ARE MOST IN CONTEXT IN A MOB;
VALIANT MEN, WHEN THEY STAND ALONE."

"THE PROBLEM WITH BRUCE JENNER
THAT IS IN NEED OF MODIFICATION IS BETWEEN
HIS EARS AND NO FURTHER SOUTH THAN THAT—
AND I DON'T THINK THAT "KEEPING-UP WITH THE
KARDASHIANS" HAS SWEETENED THE DEAL FOR
HIM ONE IOTA. FROM A WHEATIES BOX TO A BOX
OF FRUITY PEBBLES; NOW BRUCE HAS BECOME A
VERITABLE FREAK SHOW ON A HALF SHELL;
A SAD METAPHORIC POSTER CHILD FOR AN
EMASCULATED AMERICA IN CONFUSION AND
PRECIPITOUS GLOBAL DECLINE ...
HOW UTTERLY TRAGIC."

"I'VE MADE IT A POINT NOT TO SIT ON MY HANDS OR
MY INTELLECT."

"WE ARE NOT VANQUISHED BY OUR ENEMIES,
FOR OUR ENEMIES DON'T HAVE THE POWER TO
MAKE US WEAK; OUR OWN MORAL FAILINGS
ACCOMPLISH THAT."

"IF THINKING OUT-SIDE-OF-THE-BOX DOESN'T
ACTUALLY <u>GET YOU OUT</u> OF THE BOX …
YOU'RE PROBABLY SCHRÖDINGER'S CAT."

"IN MY OBSERVATIONS I PERCEIVE THAT THE
AMOUNT OF VULGARITY, OBSCENITY PROFANITY
AND BASE YOU USE AS 'AN ARTIST' IN PRODUCING
YOUR 'MUSIC,' IS IN DIRECT PROPORTION TO JUST
HOW BASE A HUMAN BEING YOU ACTUALLY ARE."

"THE WHOLE WORLD IS ON FIRE—AND EVERYONE IS
ARGUING; 'WAS IT LIGHTNING OR A MATCH?'"

"I'VE FOUND, CURIOUSLY ENOUGH, THAT
DUMPSTER PEOPLE DON'T ACTUALLY LIKE TO FIND
PEOPLE IN THEIR DUMPSTERS."

"WOMEN PROBABLY LIKE WORKING THERE,
BECAUSE THERE'S SO MANY SHINY THINGS IN
THE KITCHEN."

"IT MAY WARRANT FURTHER INVESTIGATION,
BUT I CAN'T ENVISION A SCENARIO IN WHICH
THE BUDDHA WOULD HAVE EVER NEEDED A
STUNT DOUBLE."

"HEAVEN IS A PLACE WHERE THERE IS <u>NO HOPE</u>,
NOR NEED OF IT, FOR ALL THE 'JOY UNSPEAKABLE
AND FULL OF GLORY', DESIRES AND ECSTASIES OF
REDEEMED MAN'S INFINITELY EXPANDING SPIRIT

HEART AND MIND, WILL BE MOST PERFECTLY AND
FULLY REALIZED THERE IN THE ETERNAL PRESENT
... FOREVER."

"FEAR FOR A MORTAL IS NATURAL, BUT WHEN YOU
BECOME <u>OVERLY</u> FEARFUL OF LOSING YOUR LIFE ...
YOU STOP LIVING IT."

"MAKIN' SHIT SHINE DON'T SOLVE THE PROBLEM."

"I'VE ALWAYS WORKED WITH MY HANDS;
NOW I'M TRYING TO BREAK THROUGH USING MY
MIND—AND IT'S MAKING MY HEAD HURT."

"IT'S SOON TO BE ... '<u>NOT</u> MY PROBLEM.'"

"HOW LONG CAN GOOD MEN WITNESS THE
TRIUMPH OF EVIL AND DO NOTHING
AND NOT CEASE TO BE GOOD MEN?"

"LIFE IS FULL OF TERRIBLE CHOICES THAT
HAVE TO BE MADE; SOME LEADING TO SUCCESS,
OTHERS TO FAILURE."

"I'M TRYING TO BE MANY THINGS THAT I'M NOT—
AND ALL OF THEM A BETTER MAN."

"I'M WORKING IN AN ENVIRONMENT WHERE THE
POWERS THAT BE ARE FRANTICALLY CLUTCHING
AT STRAWS—AND LAYING THEM ALL ON MY BACK."

"I GAVE A LOT MORE THAN THEY EXPECTED;
UNTIL IT GOT TO THE POINT THAT THEY EXPECTED
A WHOLE LOT MORE THAN I HAD TO GIVE."

"MUCH LIKE A NEW HAIR STYLE; IF YOU LIKE IT
BUT IT'S NOT WORKING FOR YOU,
YOU MAY NOT WANT TO EMPLOY IT."

"WHERE I WORK, IF YOU SAY—'I'VE GOT A GREAT
IDEA FOR A BETTER MOUSETRAP,' THEY'LL LOOK AT
YOU LIKE A MAN WITH THREE ASSHOLES—WHICH
INCIDENTALLY AND INTERESTINGLY ENOUGH, IS
USUALLY THE THREE GUYS I'M TALKING TO."

"<u>DON'T</u> BE THE GUY THEY INVITE TO A HAWAIIAN
LUAU AND SAY: 'OH—AND BY THE WAY, CAN YOU
BRING THE PIG?—AND I <u>DON'T</u> MEAN YOUR WIFE.'"

"IF YOU MAKE A POINT OF GOING THROUGH YOUR
LIFE ON THE CHEAP, IT WILL BE."

"I USED TO GIVE A SHIT ABOUT GIVING A SHIT;
NOW I DON'T GIVE TWO SHITS."

"LICENSE DOESN'T NEED LIBERTY TO SANCTION IT,
ONLY VIGILANCE TO TURN A BLIND EYE."

"ONLY A FOOL TAKES ADVICE FROM YES-MEN."

"ONLY THOSE WHO FIND THEMSELVES IN THE
WRONG NEED TO BE DEFENDED <u>AGAINST</u>
THE TRUTH."

"THE OVERWHELMING PHILOSOPHY OF MY NEIGHBORS ON THE LOWER EASTSIDE IS: 'WHAT'S THE POINT OF HAVING A GUN IF YOU CAN'T SHOOT IT.'"

"AS CHRISTIANS, THE ONLY BIT AND TETHER WE HAVE IS GOD THE HOLY SPIRIT."

"YOU LOSE WARS <u>IMMEDIATELY</u> WHEN YOU STOP FIGHTING THEM, NOT AFTER THE ENEMY HAS DEFEATED YOU—SO LET'S NO LONGER SAY, 'WE'RE <u>LOSING</u> THE WAR AGAINST ISIS' OR ANY SUCH ILK, FOR IF WE'RE NO LONGER FIGHTING IT; WE HAVE IN FACT, <u>ALREADY</u> LOST IT."

"THE SICKNESS OF HUMANITY CAN'T BE CURED; IT MUST BE FORGIVEN."

"IT DOESN'T MATTER IF YOU HAVE RIGHT ON YOUR SIDE; YOU MAY STILL HAVE TO FIGHT LIKE <u>THE THIRD MONKEY</u> ON NOAH'S ARK TO BE JUSTIFIED."

"THE LIFE OF THE INNOCENT IS IN THE HAND OF THE RIGHTEOUS; THE LIFE OF THE WICKED IS IN THEIR OWN HANDS."

"YOU CAN'T LIVE YOUR LIFE BY THE DREAMS OF OTHERS."

"I NEVER BRING MOONSHINE TO BIBLE STUDIES, BUT I DO TO PICNICS—AND IF A BIBLE STUDY HAPPENS TO BREAK-OUT ... OH WELL."

"WHEN IT COMES TO FOOD, IT'S ALL GOOD FOR YOU, IF YOU'RE HUNGRY AND THANKFUL FOR IT."

"THE WORLD'S GOTTEN TO BE A BALL OF MORAL INSANITY, WHICH INCIDENTALLY IS OFTEN INDISTINGUISHABLE FROM MENTAL INSANITY ... UNTIL JUDGMENT DAY."

"DEMOCRACY ONLY WORKS AND SURVIVES IF YOU HAVE AN INTELLIGENT, WELL INFORMED DISCERNING MORAL POPULACE, OTHERWISE, THE INEVITABLE DECENT INTO ANARCHY AND MOB RULE WILL UNEQUIVOCALLY BE THE ORDER OF THE DAWNING DAY."

"THESE DAYS IN AMERICA NO ONE'S WATCHING THE 'CHICKEN COOP' BUT THE 'FOXES.'"

"I DON'T THINK A MAN OUGHT TO BE KEPT DOWN BECAUSE OF THE COLOR OF HIS SKIN, NOR BE ALLOWED TO RISE BY IT."

"I SAW A GUY WALKING DOWN THE STREET TODAY THAT LOOKED JUST LIKE A SKINNY ALBERT EINSTEIN ... BUT WITHOUT THE BRAINS."

"DON'T BE SURPRISED BY PAIN; DON'T BE SURPRISED BY JOY, BECAUSE IT'S THE STUFF THAT LIFE IS MADE OF."

"NEVER SAY, 'WE SHOULD'VE DONE SOMETHING SOONER,' WHEN WE COULD DO SOMETHING <u>NOW</u>."

"Lowering the bar never closes the gap
between achievers and underachievers;
it only closes the gap between
underachievers and the ground—
aka ... 'Splat.'"

"The only thing necessary for evil to
triumph is for evil men to do nothing;
good men, would do something about it."

"Being bilingual isn't always an advantage,
if you're ignorant in both languages."

"The color of a man's skin should neither
condemn him nor justify him, but the
content of his character has power
to do both."

"The last enemy to be defeated is Death—
and if there is no resurrection,
we perish and Death wins."

"Yah I see where this thing is going,
and it's nowhere fast."

"I have some disturbing news to share,
because it's a disturbing world, full of
disturbed people, disturbing those, who
don't want to be disturbed."

"Let it go, because trying to stop it from
falling when you're drunk
will just make things worse."

"WHEN GOD CREATED AND DEFINED MARRIAGE
BETWEEN ONE MAN AND ONE WOMAN, THERE WAS
NO RELIGION, ONLY RELATIONSHIP."

"I'M NOT GOING TO START THROWING LEAD IN MY
NEIGHBORHOOD UNLESS IT'S IN DEFENSE OF MY
LIFE, OR THE INNOCENT LIVES IN PERIL THAT HAVE
NO LEAD OF THEIR OWN TO THROW."

"THE PREVAILING PHILOSOPHY APPEARS TO BE:
'DON'T WORRY ABOUT IT; LEAVE IT FOR THE NEXT
GUY—AND THE NEXT GUY'S ALWAYS ME."

"THE DIFFERENCE BETWEEN CHRISTIANS AND
NON-CHRISTIANS IS LIKE THE DIFFERENCE
BETWEEN APPLES AND ... GLORIOUS ECSTASY FOR
ETERNITY."

"IN AMERICAN GLOBAL POLITICS; THE SHOW MUST
GO ON EVEN IF THE THEATER BURNS DOWN."

"IN ANY NEW JOB THE FIRST THING YOU WANT TO
FIND OUT IS WHO'S WHO AND WHAT'S WHAT."

"THE FIRST BATTLE YOU HAVE TO WIN TO BE
VICTORIOUS IS AGAINST 'THE SELF'—
AND A MAN, WHO MASTERS HIMSELF,
IS NO SLAVE."

"AMERICAN'S ARE PLAYING AND THE REST OF THE
WORLD'S FOR REAL."

"WE AMERICANS ARE NO LONGER FREE AS I UNDERSTAND THE WORD, BUT WE HAVE A PRETTY CONVINCING ILLUSION OF IT."

"THE PROBLEM WITH DEMOCRACY IS THAT THE MOB WITH THE MAJORITY RULES—AND IF THE MOB IN MAJORITY IS BASE AND IGNORANT, THE ORDER OF THE DAY WILL BE CHAOS AND ANARCHY; WHICH INCIDENTALLY, IN NO WAY NEGATES THE FACT THAT DEMOCRACY IS WORKING."

"I'VE BEEN NOTICING FOR QUITE SOME TIME NOW, JUST HOW MANY DELIVERY SYSTEMS THERE ARE TO DELIVER THE HORROR OF HUMANITY INTO THE SANCTITY OF OUR LIVING ROOMS AND FRONT DOORS."

"I CALL MY DOCTOR 'DOC HOLLIDAY,' BECAUSE I CAN NEVER GET A HOLD OF HIM FOR AN APPOINTMENT; HE'S ALWAYS INCOMMUNICADO ON A VACATION—AND HE'S NOWHERE TO BE FOUND."

"HAVE YOU EVER NOTICED WHEN YOU'RE DRIVING TO GET SOMEWHERE FAST, THAT YOU'RE QUITE CERTAIN THE GUY RIDING YOUR ASS IS ON CRACK OR METH, WHILE THE DUDE IN FRONT OF YOU IS POPPIN' QUAALUDES OR WASHING-DOWN XANAX® WITH JOHNNIE WALKERS RED?"

"SOME MEN SUCCEED EVEN WHILE THEY'RE FAILING; OTHERS FAIL IN THE MIDST OF THEIR SUCCESS."

"EVERYONE'S LOOKING FOR THEIR FIFTEEN MINUTES OF FAME; WHICH IS TANTAMOUNT TO

BEING ONE OF THE MOST POPULAR AND INFLUENTIAL RATS ON A SINKING SHIP."

"ALL MEN ARE CREATED EQUAL (IN THAT THEY ARE CREATED FREE), BUT NOT ALL MEN REMAIN EQUAL FOR SOME ARE ENSLAVED—AND SETTING A SLAVE AT LIBERTY FROM HIS BONDAGE MAKES HIM FREE, THOUGH NOT AT ONCE EQUAL WITH ALL OTHER MEN; EQUALITY HE MUST EARN, FOR THE EARNEST DESIRE TO GIVE HIM FREELY WHAT HE MUST GAIN FOR HIMSELF, WILL NEVER MAKE HIM EQUAL WITH THOSE NEVER ENSLAVED."

"PAL, I'M NOT YOUR AVERAGE ANYTHING, EVEN THOUGH I CAN'T ALWAYS PROVE IT."

"I LIKE TO BELIEVE I HAVE MORE TO OFFER THAN JUST MY TIME ON THE CLOCK."

"NOBODY'LL GIVE A SHIT ABOUT THE SHIT YOUR SAYIN' IF YOU'RE ALWAYS TALKING SHIT."

"THIS USED TO BE AMERICA, BUT WE'VE GOTTEN OVER IT."

"SOMETIMES AN ITCH YOU CAN'T SCRATCH ONCE YOU FINALLY GET TO IT; TURNS OUT NOT TO BE AN ITCH AT ALL."

"SOME PEOPLE THINK THEY SHOULD BE GIVEN FREELY THE THINGS THEY DON'T HAVE JUST BECAUSE THEY WANT THEM—AND OTHER FOLKS AGREE; THOSE WHO AGREE ARE CALLED LIBERALS."

"America is no longer 'half slave and half free;' the slaves emancipated for over a century and a half from their <u>masters</u> are now free men and women. <u>They are the masters of their own destiny</u>—and if they're yet unequal, they must address the shortfall with their <u>current masters</u>."

"A false prophet must be able to lie with equal enthusiasm about both God and the devil to be successful in his craft—and it's <u>always</u> simultaneously."

"The world has built for itself a house of cards in a wind tunnel, with the switch in God's hand on a timer."

"One can't change God's narrative of the future ... only fulfill it."

"We do pretty much what we want to do because humanity has never taken "No!" for an answer."

"For too many, peace is a foreign country—and a land far away."

"If it's a choice between being a dog person and a cat person ...
I'll take the peregrine falcon every time."

"I've come to realize that bouncing a corrupt career politician decisively to the curb asshole over tin cup is like trying to wipe your ass with wax paper."

"You can't always say
'See ya in the mornin,'
because not everyone wakes up."

"At this point does anyone <u>really</u> think
there's nothing wrong with humanity
that <u>we can't</u> fix?"

"If he brushes his teeth with meth and
flosses with razor wire—
you'll definitely want to steer
clear of his wife."

"The world will soon become an asylum
that everyone wants to get out of …
except for the insane."

"No; a <u>big</u> spider's one that's outgrown
its leash."

"What part of 'Be very careful,
they're very sharp,'
<u>didn't</u> you understand—
and by the way …
<u>don't</u> push that red button."

"They say 'you can't come home'—
and it's true, if you come back as a self-
absorbed arrogant jackass."

"Sometimes the only thing the innocent are
guilty of is being innocent."

"IF YOU'RE GOING TO TAKE FROM THE RICH
AND GIVE TO THE POOR; LEAVE THE MIDDLE
CLASS OUT OF IT."

"DON'T CUT YOURSELF AND THEN ASK—
'WHY WAS THE KNIFE SO SHARP?'"

"IT'S NOT THE GUY DRIVING IN FRONT OF ME THAT
CONCERNS ME; IT'S THE ACCRUED, UNOCCUPIED
THIRTY CAR LENGTHS IN FRONT OF THE GUY
DRIVING IN FRONT OF ME THAT BOILS MY ONIONS."

"BREASTS OR THIGHS IT'S ALL THE SAME TO THE
FOX … AND TO THE CHICKEN."

"MIGHT THE LORD ALWAYS PULL YOU BACK FROM
THE EDGE AND KEEP YOU ON THE COOL SIDE OF
THE FIRE LINE."

"VAPID GRINNING JACKASSES AND OBNOXIOUS
ARROGANT BLOWHARDS ARE THE SUM OF ALL
FEARS IN MODERN AMERICA POLITICS."

"I PERCEIVE THE WORLD ADRIFT; A BUBBLE
FLOATING INTO A PATCH OF
MID-SUMMER THISTLE."

"THERE'S ONLY A RIGHT AND NOT A WRONG PLACE
TO HIDE, FOR IF YOU'RE HIDDEN AND YOU WANT TO
BE HIDDEN, THEN YOU'RE IN THE RIGHT PLACE; IF
YOU WANT TO BE HIDDEN AND IT'S IN THE WRONG
PLACE, THEN YOU'RE NOT HIDDEN."

"I FIND IT'S ONLY 'QUITE A DELICIOUS DILEMMA,'
IF IT'S <u>NOT</u> ON <u>YOUR</u> PLATE."

"'CHAFF' HAS NO PLACE OF HONOR; IT MUST BE
WINNOWED OUT AND BLOWN AWAY."

"IT'LL ALL CHANGE FOR AMERICA WHEN THE
WHEELS COME OFF THE BUS ON THE TRACKS."

"MAN WASN'T THERE WHEN GOD CREATED,
BUT HE'LL BE HERE WHEN GOD DESTROYS."

"GOD'S DECISIONS AND DECREES ARE NOT
SUBJECT TO REVIEW."

"THE WHOLE WORLD IS HEADING FOR "SPLAT!"—
AND IN GOD'S ECONOMY, SPLAT …
<u>IS</u> ALSO A FOUR-LETTER WORD."

"I LIKE WHAT IT SAYS ABOUT MY BOSS,
THAT HE'D RATHER CATCH HIS GUYS WORKING,
THAN NOT WORKING."

"EVIL IS A THING NOT TO BE UNDERSTOOD;
IT MUST BE EXPLAINED AWAY."

"I WISH I COULD WEAR THOSE MUSCLE SHIRTS
LIKE SOME GUYS—BUT THEN, I'D HAVE TO GET
SOME MUSCLES."

"OUR HUMANITY IS UP FOR GRABS—
AND I SEE NO SOFT LANDING IN OUR FUTURE."

"WE'VE ALWAYS GONE GREEN WHERE I WORK;
EVERYTHING RUNS ON MASSIVE AMOUNTS OF PURE
ECO-FRIENDLY EGO."

"SINCE THE SUPREME COURT'S CONTROVERSIAL
'GAY MARRIAGE' DECREE, THEY'RE ALL OUT THERE
AND LOVING IT—AND NOT TO BE OUT-DONE,
THE HOUSING INDUSTRY IS NO LONGER BUILDING
HOMES WITH CLOSETS."

"AMERICA THE ONCE AWAKENED 'SLEEPING
GIANT,' HAS MORPHED ITSELF GLOBALLY INTO A
STUMBLEBUM GIANT, BUT A GIANT, IS ONLY A
GIANT ... UNTIL HE HITS THE GROUND."

"DON'T THINK THAT YOU'RE IN GOOD HEALTH JUST
BECAUSE YOU'RE PAIN FREE,
HAPPY AND FEELING GREAT; DOCTORS CAN
CHANGE ALL THAT IN AN INSTANT."

"KNOWING THE DIFFERENCE BETWEEN SHIT AND
SHOESHINE ONLY MATTERS
IF YOU'VE GOT SHINE-ABLE SHOES."

"PLAYING THE RACE CARD IS A TWO-EDGED
SWORD—AND ONLY WORKS UNTIL YOUR
PARTICULAR RACE FALLS INTO DISFAVOR."

"IT'S NOT A GESTURE OF DISRESPECT, BUT I
WOULDN'T EVEN GO TO MY OWN FUNERAL IF
I DIDN'T HAVE TO."

"THERE IS A BEAUTY THAT TRANSCENDS PHYSICAL
BEAUTY AND EMBRACES THE DIVINE."

"Like my old Granddaddy once told me:
'Son; you just can't go off shootin' the one-
legged man because he didn't win the ass-
kickin' contest.'"

"People are like wine, in that all wines have
parentage and a past, but only GREAT
'wines' ... have a future."

"Too many are dissatisfied and jaded
because people are looking for a lifestyle,
not a life."

"Remember: the left-handed monkey wrench
is always next to the skyhook—
and right in front of the bucket of sparks."

"I've found that matters can be very
slippery things when you take them into
your own hands."

"The whole world's a stage of actors—and
it's not the end of the world yet,
but the Gaffers have arrived; pulling
electrical cables from the set."

"If the first kick of the mule doesn't clear
your head and cause you to focus;
the second kick would be superfluous."

"Fostering an unforgiving spirit and
holding grudges is like having a conjoined
twin that has died—and only forgiving them
will deliver you from this body of death and

THE EXHAUSTING POISONOUS BURDEN YOU FACE;
FAR BETTER TO FORGIVE AND CUT THEM LOOSE …
<u>SO YOU MIGHT BOTH BE SET FREE</u>.”

“I AND A FAMOUS FRIEND OF MINE WENT TO A
GREAT RUSTIC BAR NEAR HIS HOMETOWN ONE
AFTERNOON—AND WHEN HE INTRODUCED HIMSELF
TO THE BARTENDER THE GUY SAID:
‘YOU MENTION YOUR LAST NAME IN HERE PAL
AND YOU’LL NEVER PAY FOR A DRINK—
AND WHEN I LET HIM KNOW WHO I WAS HE
REPLIED: ‘AND YOU TELL-UM YOUR NAME AROUND
HERE … YOU’LL NEVER GET A DRINK.’”

“YAH, MY PHYSICAL WENT PRETTY WELL I GUESS,
BUT BOY, AM I GETTIN’ TO HATE THOSE QUARTERLY
PROSTATE EXAMS MY DOCTOR KEEPS
SCHEDULING; EVERY YEAR IT’S THE SAME THING—
TURN AROUND, BEND OVER, SPREAD YOUR
CHEEKS, HERE COMES THE LUBE AND RELAX—IT’S
THE LONGEST FIVE MINUTES OF MY LIFE THAT I
KNOW I’M NOT GETTIN’ BACK.” ‘OH DUDE!’ …
‘SERIOUSLY?’ … ‘I DON’T THINK THAT’S A
PROSTATE EXAM YOU’VE BEEN GETTING.’”

“AMERICA HAS EXTRACTED, EXACTED,
SQUANDERED AND EXTRUDED THE WEALTH OF
NATIONS … ESPECIALLY OUR OWN.”

“CONGRESS AND THE SENATE ARE FULL OF ‘I FEEL
YOUR PAIN’ ‘ROGERS,’ BUT WE’RE PLUMB OUT OF
‘DONE AND DONE!’ ‘WILCOS.’”

“NOBODY NEEDS A GOD THAT’S ONLY AS SMART
AS HIS PROPHET.”

"WAIT FOR IT ... SOON THE WHOLE CAREFUL
STRICTURE OF THIS FRAGILE WORLD
WILL SHATTER LIKE CRYSTAL ON CONCRETE."

"YOU'VE GOT TO PARDON ME, BUT I'VE GOT A LOT
ON MY MIND AND NONE OF IT'S YOU."

"FREEDOM IS NOT CARTE BLANCHE, BUT THE
PURSUIT OF MAINTAINING COSTLY LIBERTY BY WAY
OF ETERNAL VIGILANCE AND THE APPLIED PRICE
OF FREEDOM UNDERSTOOD."

"MODERN AMERICA IS ONE OF THE FEW PLACES
THE DYSFUNCTIONAL ARE ALLOWED TO THRIVE
UNMOLESTED IN THEIR CATCH-AS-CATCH-CAN
WORLD, BECAUSE WE REFUSE TO HOLD THEM
ACCOUNTABLE TO THE COLLECTIVE, WHICH MAKES
US COMPLICIT IN THEIR DYSFUNCTION BY GRACING
IT WITH OUR OWN."

"I GUESS, I DON'T KNOW, O.K., WHATEVER, WE'LL
SEE—IS NOT THE ANSWER YOU WANT TO HEAR
FOLLOWING... 'WILL YOU MARRY ME?'"

"NO, OFFICER, I'M NOT DRUNK, IN FACT, CAN'T WE
JUST AGREE THAT I'M STAYING THOROUGHLY
HYDRATED AND EXTREMELY RELAXED WHILE
DRIVING?"

"PLATINUM, GOLD, SILVER, CLAY;
GOD CAN WORK WITH AND THROUGH ANY VESSEL,
AS LONG AS IT'S CLEAN."

"I USED TO HANG WITH A LOT OF FRIENDS THAT'RE STILL REMODELING THE INSIDE OF THEIR HEADS WITH CANNABIS."

"ABORTION IS WRONG—BECAUSE IF HUMAN LIFE IS CHEAP IN THE WOMB, IT WILL BE CHEAP TO THE TOMB."

"MY CLAIM TO FAME IS; THAT I'VE LEARNED WELL, WHAT I HAVEN'T BEEN TAUGHT."

"I ONCE ASKED MYSELF, 'WHY IS EVERYONE BUYING UP AMERICA?'—AND THEN IT OCCURRED TO ME ... BECAUSE IT'S FOR SALE—'DUH!'"

"FAITH TAKES COURAGE—AND FAITH LIKE COURAGE IS A CHOICE."

"WE KEEP-ON THINKING THAT REALITY IS WHAT IT ONCE WAS, BUT THE NATURE OF REALITY DOESN'T CHANGE—AND IT ALWAYS IS WHAT IT IS RIGHT NOW."

"JUST BECAUSE YOU MAY NOT HAVE AN ISSUE WITH DRUGS AND ALCOHOL DOESN'T MEAN YOU DON'T STILL HAVE A PROBLEM WITH THEM."

"FOR SOME PEOPLE THEIR FIRST NO IS THEIR FINAL NO TO GOD; FOR OTHERS ... IT IS THEIR LAST."

"I DON'T TRUST LAWYERS BECAUSE YOU CAN'T TRUST ANYONE WHO CAN SING WITHOUT

COMPUNCTION AND WITH EQUAL ENTHUSIASM,
BOTH THE BATTLE HYMN OF THE REPUBLIC
AND DIXIE."

"SOMETIMES IN AMERICA THE WILL OF THE
PEOPLE IS CONTRARY TO THEIR BEST INTERESTS—
BUT RARELY AS OFTEN AS THEIR LEADERS THINK."

"WHEN THE APOCALYPSE COMES—AND YOU RUN
OUT OF FOOD, JUST LOOK AT THE BRIGHT SIDE;
NOBODY'LL BE COMING TO YOUR HOUSE FOR
DINNER ... OH YAH, UNLESS OF COURSE ...
THEY'RE ZOMBIES."

"I DON'T LIGHT A CANDLE OR PRAY
FOR THE DEAD, BUT FOR THE LIVING—
THAT THEY MIGHT REMAIN SO."

"ANYONE WHO'S BEEN WATCHING KNOWS;
THE SUBTEXT OF HUMANITY IS ONE OF HORROR."

"IF THEY EVER SAY: 'WE WANT TO TAKE <u>IN GOD
WE TRUST</u> OFF OF OUR U.S. MONEY' ...
I'LL SAY, 'WHY NOT?' ... BECAUSE <u>WE DON'T</u>."

"AMERICA CONTINUES TO CALL UPON HER HEROES
TO BE HEROIC ... BUT <u>ONLY</u> ... <u>HER HEROES</u>."

"I'VE OFTEN PAID A PRICE FOR DOING WHAT'S
RIGHT; MERCIFULLY, NOT ALWAYS FOR DOING
WHAT'S WRONG."

"IN GOD'S ECONOMY, PRIDE AND ARROGANCE;
SELF-PITY AND SELF-DEPRECATION—
ARE NO MAN'S LAND."

"<u>OVERSIGHT OF PREVENTIVE MAINTENANCE</u> IS
EXCEEDINGLY IMPORTANT—AND JUST BECAUSE
YOU FIND YOURSELF RUNNING AROUND ALL DAY
PUTTING OUT FIRES THAT SHOULD'VE <u>NEVER</u> BEEN
STARTED, <u>DOESN'T</u> MAKE YOU A GOOD
SUPERVISOR OF THE AFOREMENTIONED."

"THEY SAY THAT: 'EVERYTHING LOOKS BETTER IN
THE LIGHT OF DAY' ... EXCEPT OF COURSE,
FOR BATTLEFIELDS AND UGLY WOMEN."

"I OFTEN WRITE BECAUSE I NEED TO HEAR WHAT
I HAVE TO SAY."

"SOME PEOPLE NEVER WORRY ABOUT PLUGGING
THE 'LEAKS' IN THEIR LIVES, BECAUSE THEY KNOW
IF THEY JUST LEAVE THEM ALONE LONG ENOUGH,
THEY'LL EVENTUALLY CORRUPT—AND ROT
THEMSELVES SHUT."

"YAH, I KNOW THE RODENTIA FAMILY;
THEY USED TO LIVE ON THE LOWER EAST SIDE
BEFORE THEY MOVED TO LITTLE ITALY ON THE
WEST SIDE ... BIG FAMILY ... LOVED THE CHEESE,
PEPERONI AND PEANUT BUTTER!"

"STICKS AND STONES; SWORDS AND ARROWS;
NUKES AND DRONES; SANITIZED OR NO, LET
THEIR LIFE BLOOD FLOW; WAR, WILL MAN
<u>NEVER LET GO</u>."

"SO, TELL ME SUPERINTENDENT—
WHY DO <u>YOU</u> THINK SEX EDUMAKATION ISN'T
WORKING IN THE PUBLIC-SCHOOL SYSTEM?"

"THE DIE IS CAST; THE PROPHECIES HAVE BEEN
SPOKEN; THE HANDWRITING IS ON THE WALL …
'IT IS FINISHED.'"

"DIAMONDS, PLATINUM, GOLD AND SILVER ONLY
HAVE VALUE IN A SOCIETY AND WORLD THAT STILL
HAS HOPE."

"BEING A DRUG ADDICT DOESN'T ABSOLVE YOU OF
THE CRIMES OF NECESSITY YOU'VE COMMITTED IN
GETTING THERE."

"THERE ARE PERNICIOUS THINGS THAT GOD
DOESN'T WANT US TRYING OR ACCESSING
BECAUSE HE KNOWS IF WE DO, WE'LL LIKE THEM."

"IF YOU'RE MARRYING THE SICILIAN GODFATHER'S
DAUGHTER—AND HE TAKES YOU ASIDE AT THE
REHEARSAL DINNER, PUTS HIS ARM AROUND YOUR
NECK AND WHISPERS IN YOUR EAR: 'KID, DON'T
EVER GET A VASECTOMY.' I'D SHY AWAY FROM
TELLING HIM … 'OH DUDE!' I WOULD NEVER THINK
OF GETTING MY "JUNK" SNIPPED—AND BESIDES
THAT POPS … I MIGHT WANNA-HAVE KIDS WITH MY
NEXT WIFE.'"

"MATURITY IS TO COME TO THE PLACE WHERE ONE
CAN SAY: 'IT'S NOT AS SIMPLE AND BENIGN A
WORLD AS I ONCE THOUGHT IT WAS.'"

"It wouldn't do for the Church to close its doors and think it's safe within; when the power once purchased and bequeathed is to be wielded in the battle outside the doors."

"You don't need a wingman supporting you when you're doing what's wrong."

"If you're base in the company of people who have no human decency, you'll never notice—and you'll offend no one."

"A once free mind can only remain swaddled as long as it doesn't know that it is."

"Once I convinced myself I was a writer I found it a lot easier to write."

"Writing can be like a figure skater in early spring skating on a lake of thin ice."

"As regards and explains the assigning of blame to our President for not prosecuting the war against I.S.I.S. and other terrorists—"The _onus_ for the _modus_ is on the _Potus_ who's a _lotus_.""

"You can't be or do anything you want, but you can be and do, many things you don't."

"Being pessimistic doesn't make it untrue."

"THINGS ONLY GET WORSE BECAUSE <u>SOMEBODY</u>
MADE IT NECESSARY."

"I ALWAYS THOUGHT I WAS TALL, UNTIL I WALKED
IN FRONT OF A FULL-LENGTH MIRROR WITH SOME
OF MY FRIENDS THAT WERE."

"I LIKE LOOKING THINGS UP, BECAUSE I LIKE TO
KNOW HOW THINGS WORK—FOR EXAMPLE …
WORDS."

"THE THING MERCHANTS OF CORPORATE AMERICA
SELL FAR BETTER THAN ANYTHING ELSE IS
DISSATISFACTION IN THE STATUS QUO."

"REGARDING MY CURRENT JOB; I'D PREFER TO
MAKE A LIVING <u>NOT</u> BEING THERE."

"IN DIRE STRAITS ONE MUST HAVE HOPE
BEYOND THE HORROR."

"<u>A DRONE</u>, IS A MALE HONEYBEE THAT DOESN'T
WORK BUT CAN STILL MATE WITH THE QUEEN, AN
UNMANNED AERIAL VEHICLE, OR—
AN 'UNMANNED WOMEN.'"

"FROM HIGH SCHOOL SOME WILL GO ON TO
COLLEGES WHERE THEY'LL BE TAUGHT NOT TO
THINK FOR THEMSELVES—AND BECOME FURTHER
'EDUCATED' BEYOND THEIR ABILITY OR NEED TO
REASON."

"BE ADVISED: 'GETTING AWAY WITH IT IS ONLY A
TEMPORARY CONDITION.'"

"ALL CONGRESS NEEDS TO BREAK THE GRIDLOCK
IS MORE FIBER IN ITS DIET."

"SOMEONE WAS ONCE THE CATALYST IN OUR LIVES
THAT CHANGED THE TRAJECTORY FOR GOOD, OR
FOR EVIL."

"WHEN I WAS YOUNG THINGS WERE ALL EXCITING
AND NEW; NOW THINGS ARE ALL DIFFERENT …
BUT NOTHING IS NEW."

"ENDEAVOR TO BE A PERSON OF SIGNIFICANCE
AND A TARGET OF HIGH VALUE,
BECAUSE NOBODY EVER NOTICES AN EMPTY
APPLECART BEING UPENDED."

"THE WORLD IS FULL OF THE BASE …
NOT SO MUCH THE SUBLIME."

"YOU'LL HAVE TO EXCUSE ME, BUT I'M FACING IN
THE WRONG DIRECTION FOR IT TO BE MORNING."

"SOME NAVIGATE BY THE STARS; SOME BY THE
BARS; OTHERS BY THEIRS SCARS."

"NO, I BELIEVE HIS FULL GIVEN NAME IS—BARACK
NEVILLE HUSSAIN CHAMBERLAIN OBAMA."

"Far too many as soon as they're challenged or perceive a slight, immediately retreat to the comfort of <u>their safe place</u>; snug and secure under the cover of the ever-thickening and all-enveloping blanket of <u>the race card</u>."

"I would much prefer an incompetent to a coward in the office of the Presidency or any other high office, for incompetence can be compensated for; cowardice … cannot."

"In too many venues these days; there's no accountants; there's no accounting; there's no accountability."

"Let's compromise, the name Washington Redskins stays, but we change the name of the Dallas Cowboys or New England Patriots to the Palefaces."

"The radical social movements in America are emboldened because they smell blood in the water; they just don't know that it's their own."

"It's gotten to be a dog-eat-dog world—and even the "dogs" are gettin' knocked of the gut-wagons with indigestion."

"Monsters and Goliaths in our lives are not easily converted; we must flee them or destroy them."

"You're really quite right; I really 'don't know nothing,' I know a great deal, in fact."

"You can't say to America 'stay the course' <u>if you have no plan</u>, nor 'steady as she goes' while she's sinking beneath the waves into a crushing black oblivion."

"I am who I am because I've been standing on the shoulders of Giants ... and they're starting to get pissed-off."

"I think I'm going to start paying my memories forward."

"A posture of prayer is the condition of the heart, not the positioning of the body."

"Being a writer, I'm always striving to articulate words more betterly."

"Humanity can't look to itself for deliverance, only temporary reprieves."

"<u>Lichens</u>" are those leechlike parasitic creatures in America that are likin' the fact they don't have to work to eat or pay to play—and likin' the fact Uncle Sam's footing the bill for it all."

"One must come to realize; a rehydrated turd is still just a turd."

"'Rest in peace' or 'Rot in purgatory;'
R.I.P. can be somewhat ambiguous to all
but the departed."

"God created everything including
creativity."

"I would rather spend my life creating,
than managing chaos."

"If you say things you don't have to defend;
they're probably things that aren't worth
defending."

"A word to the young: 'If you're going to
screw up your life wait till you're rich.'"

"I hope it all ends before I do."

"Now don't go pushin' me around,
cus I'll have you know;
I have high friends in a lot of places."

"If you can utter it, someone's probably
been named it."

"God lays me down to sleep with sweet
thoughts of victory; Satan startles me
awake with the dread of defeat."

"CONSIDERING THE NATURE AND CONTENT OF MY WRITING, I PERCEIVE MY BRAIN REPLETE WITH MORE THAN MERE PHYSICAL CONVOLUTIONS."

"AMERICA IS ON ITS WAY OUT; THE ONLY QUESTION IS, WHICH EXIT STRATEGY ARE WE GOING TO EMPLOY?"

"I'VE FOUND THAT THE DIFFERENCE BETWEEN A DRUNKEN BUM AND A BUMMING DRUNK IS REALLY QUITE NEGLIGIBLE."

"DON'T BE AFRAID OF REALITY ...
IT'S ALL WE'VE GOT."

"AMERICANS HAVE BECOME A NATION OF LOTUS-EATERS IN A WORLD THAT HAS A TASTE FOR BLOOD."

"ONE MUST RESPECT OTHERS; UNLESS OF COURSE THEY INSIST UPON PERSUADING YOU OTHERWISE."

"THERE'S NOTHING WRONG WITH PUTTING ALL YOUR EGGS IN ONE BASKET
IF ALL YOU'VE GOT IS ONE BASKET."

"'... AND <u>A LITTLE CHILD</u> SHALL LEAD THEM.'—NOT THE MONSTERS OF MECHANIZED DEATH RIDING ATOP THEIR TANKS, OR THE ARROGANT YET CRAVEN POTENTATES IN POMP AND LAUD, NOR THE LORDS OF WAR WITH THEIR FINGER HOVERING OVER A NUCLEAR TRIGGER ... '<u>A LITTLE CHILD</u> SHALL LEAD THEM.'"

"REGARDING AMERICAN'S POLICY ON TERRORISM;
IT IS WHAT IT IS; WE'LL CHANGE IT NEXT TIME,
BUT WE'RE NOT GOING TO DO ANYTHING ABOUT
THIS TIME."

"WE'RE LIVING IN A WORLD FULL OF VICTIMS
IGNORING THEIR TURN."

"IN THESE DAYS I CAN BELIEVE MORE AND MORE
WHAT I'VE NEVER BELIEVED BEFORE."

"IT'S GOOD TO WORK WITHOUT PAIN;
EPICALLY IF HE'S A PAIN IN THE ASS."

"THEY HEAR WHAT THEY WANT TO HEAR, BECAUSE
WHAT I SAID IS: 'YOU'RE A RETARD AND AN ASS-
HEAD'—WHAT HE HEARD WAS; 'YOU'RE A
RESOURCE AND AN ASSET.'"

"I STRONGLY PERCEIVE THAT ALL THE CANDIDATES
CURRENTLY RUNNING IN THIS RACE ARE
<u>EMINENTLY QUALIFIED</u> TO BE PRESIDENT OF OUR
FAILING AND FADING; FALLING ON OUR FACE FROM
GRACE DYSFUNCTIONAL, U.S. OF A."

"AMERICA NO LONGER HAS THE LUXURY
OF MERELY ROUNDING-UP THE USUAL SUSPECTS
IN OUR WAR AGAINST TERROR; NOW WE HAVE TO
BE ROUSTING THE 'HOME-GROWNS'—SALLY, DICK
AND JIHADI JANE."

"I THINK I'M IN THE WRONG FREAKIN' CENTURY,
BUT I'M NOT SURE WHICH ONE."

"It never ceases to amaze me how far a beautiful woman can go in this world with nothing more than a butt-thong and a smile."

"Like Annette Funicello, Britney Spears was never a Playboy bunny, she was a Mouseketeer—a rodent with much smaller ears."

"An obedient Christian living their life daily by degrees is just a martyr in slow motion."

"'Monsters' have always created the reality in which all of us must live."

"If your wife can't cook, 'A bird in the hand' is <u>still</u> 'worth two in the bush'."

"In Christian parlance: They that have 'the disease,' but harbor contempt for the cure—will never be healed."

"The link between possibility and reality is permission; that which we give ourselves—and that of Providence."

"I've not been gifted for naught."

"You can't be humble and arrogant at the same time, but you can be humble and bold."

"The downside of being a go-to-guy is you're always gone to."

"Like our President 'waging' what passes for 'war' in his mind and parlance against the terrorists of ISIS and other maniacal Muslims; 'Burning one's tidy-whities so they're no longer contagious is addressing, but not solving the problem.'"

"I'm sorry, but I only speak through my Attorneys from the esteemed law offices of—Saynuttin, Tilleye and Sayso."

"I never buy suits off the rack; they're custom-tailored and finely fitted for me by the exquisite couturiers of Hulk & Lurch."

"We <u>get to be</u> strong to bear the weaknesses of the weak."

"Old, tired, alone and ready to go home, is a good day to die."

"They have no identities, so they identify with each other ... which makes them nobodies."

"If a paradigm is continuously shifting, its definition of necessity must be changed as well."

"A DUMB-ASS IS SOMEONE WHO SUFFERS A
SIGNIFICANT LOSS OF BRAIN CELLS
EVERY TIME THEY TAKE A SHIT."

"NONE OF US WITH THE REMOTE IN OUR HAND CAN
AFFECT OR TOUCH THE PRESENT, NOR CHANGE
THE FUTURE ... BUT MERELY ACCESS THE PAST."

"IN THE FUTURE NOBODY'S GOING TO GET WHAT
THEY WANT; ESPECIALLY THOSE WHO MADE SUCH
A FUTURE POSSIBLE."

"FANTASY CAN BE MORE PLEASING THAN A
REALITY THAT DOESN'T EXIST."

"I'D BE TERRIFIED TO LIVE MY LIFE AS IF THERE
WERE NO GOD, NOR DAY OF RECKONING."

"ALWAYS QUICKLY REACT TO THE REACTION
TO THE ACTION."

"AS AMERICANS, '<u>TAKING</u> OUR COUNTRY BACK' IS
NOT THE ANSWER; <u>PUTTING</u> IT BACK IN THE HAND
OF KIND PROVIDENCE IS."

"LIKING IT DOESN'T MAKE IT LEGIT NOR
NEGATE ITS LEGITIMACY."

"THE MOST TERRIFYING PLACE ON EARTH IS,
WHEREVER YOU ARE WHEN IT HAPPENS TO YOU."

"LOOKY-HERE AND CONSIDER WHAT I SAY; FOOD
AND ENTERTAINMENT IS THE FABRIC OF OUR
LIVES—AND WHAT MAKES THE WORLD-GO-ROUND."

"I HAVE A MORAL STREAK RUNNING THROUGH ME
THE BURNS MY SOUL AND WON'T ALLOW ME TO BE
HAPPY AS A LESSER MAN."

"YOU MIGHT AS WELL BE BRAVE, BECAUSE
NOBODY WANTS TO DIE; ALL WANT TO LIVE—AND
BEING A COWARD DOESN'T CHANGE THAT."

"TRIPPING OVER A BUCKET OF LIGHT IN THE
DARKNESS IS THE LEGACY OF HUMANITY."

"THERE'S LESS CHANCE OF SHOOTIN' SOMEBODY
IF YOU DON'T HAVE A GUN,
BUT MORE CHANCE OF GETTIN' SHOT."

"MOST DON'T SEE SIN FOR WHAT IT IS,
OR THE ENEMY FOR WHO HE IS."

"I'M AT THE POINT IN MY LIFE WHERE I DON'T
WANT TO HUSTLE ANYMORE PHYSICALLY,
BUT INTELLECTUALLY."

"WHERE'D I HEAR THAT YOU ASK ... I WROTE IT,
SO I HEAR IT EVERY TIME I QUOTE MYSELF."

"I'D MUCH PREFER TO EARN MY LIVING
CREATING, THAN MERELY MANAGING AND
MITIGATING DESTRUCTION."

"THE INTERNET CAN'T MAKE YOU SMART,
ONLY DEPENDENT."

"FAILURE IS NEVER HAVING DONE
ANYTHING NOBLE WITH WHAT YOU'VE CREATED
OR BEEN GIVEN."

"IT'S NICE TO BE ACKNOWLEDGED AND
APPRECIATED, BUT THE LAST THING
I WANT TO HEAR COMING FROM MY BOSS IS …
'YAH GIVE ME A CHANCE TO WIPE MY ASS,
AND I'LL BE RIGHT OUT TO SHAKE YOUR HAND.'"

"IN AMERICA YOU'RE LIKELY TO FIND MANY
WOMEN GREAT WITH CHILD …
AND MANY MORE GREAT, WITHOUT."

"THE ONLY SWORD IMPOSSIBLE TO SHARPEN IS
THE ONE THAT'S ALREADY SHARP."

"THE BEST LEADERS ARE THOSE WHO
DELEGATE <u>AND</u> FACILITATE."

"THERE ARE NO DISEMBODIED SPIRITS BUT IN
HEAVEN OR HELL—AND ONLY DEMONS AMONG THE
LIVING MASQUERADING AS SUCH."

"LIFE CAN BE A DAUNTING AND OVERWHELMING
PROPOSITION, SO THE ONLY THING I WANT TO SEE
ON MY PLATE FROM NOW ON IS MY SUPPER."

"DON'T LET YOURSELF BE DEFINED OR INVENTED
BY SOMEONE ELSE."

"What I've accomplished today was not
being at work."

"You know you're good when you start
taking notes on yourself."

"You know you've got a big rat problem
when the rats aren't getting caught
in the traps, the traps are getting caught
in the rats."

"I don't know what kind of weather's in the
forecast, but I sure hope I am."

"Humanity is hollowing itself out that it
might fill itself up."

"Where I work nobody cares about it until
you don't care about it—
then everyone cares about it."

"Government can't change human behavior,
only restrain it, or unleash it."

"If you keep claiming that you're a victim
and not equal, eventually you'll be
believed—and treated accordingly."

"Have you noticed how full the world is of
people who are always trying
to beat you to the next red light?"

"I HAVE TO HAND IT TO HOLLYWOOD AND GREAT ACTING; THE MOVIE *INSOMNIA* MAKES ME TIRED, AND THE MOVIE *FARGO* MAKES ME COLD."

"WHERE I WORK THE MOTTO IS: 'JUST MAKE IT HAPPEN!'—BECAUSE IF YOU SUCCEED, YOU'RE NO HERO, BUT IF YOU FAIL … YOU'RE THE VILLAIN."

"'MORE!' IS THE CLARION CALL OF HUMANITY."

"I'D RATHER SUCCEED BY DESIGN,
THAN WIN BY CHANCE."

"ANYONE CAN BE A VICTIM;
IT TAKES COURAGE TO BE FREE."

"EVERY MAN WANTS TO BE A HERO …
IT'S 'THE GOD GENE'…
'FOR WE'RE ALSO HIS OFFSPRING…'"

"THIN SKIN AND A THICK SKULL ARE THE MAKINGS FOR A VERY VULNERABLE LIFE."

"RULES ARE MADE TO BE BROKEN AND CONSEQUENCES MEANT TO BE THE CONSEQUENCES THEREOF."

"THEY SAY THERE'S NOTHING NEW UNDER THE SUN, EXCEPT OF COURSE AT TIMES, THAT SUSPICIOUS LOOKING MOLE CANNIBALIZING YOUR FACE."

"The first recorded robbery
in humanity's history was that of
Cain taking what didn't belong to him …
the life of his brother Abel."

"Rest is the catalyst for creativity,
as surely as leisure time is the mother
of invention."

"I make no excuses for political
correctness, nor apologies for the truth."

"Note to self:
'All I really want is what I don't have.'"

"God never gets more glory or less glory …
'He gets all glory.'"

"The last thing you want to be doing is
dancing a dance to nowhere with someone
you love."

"If you want job security, become a Shrink,
because from what I can see, the world's
never going to run-out of 'shrinkies.'"

"'Cotton is king'—and the king deposed is
dust—and like cotton, dust is eventually the
fabric of our lives."

"Modern humans are living their lives as an
extension of their cell phones;
a willing appendage to their devices."

"'XANAX®-IT' AND GET OVER IT, BECAUSE IN RUSH-HOUR BIG CITY GRIDLOCK, <u>EVERYONE</u> FEELS LIKE A FART TRAPPED BEHIND A TURD."

"I WANT MY LIFE TO BE BETTER NOT MERELY DIFFERENT, BECAUSE ONE'S LIFE CAN BE DIFFERENT IN MANY WAYS—AND STILL BE VERY UNPLEASANT."

"MUCH LIKE THIS QUOTE,
IT'S ALL ABOUT THE CREATIVE PROCESS
AND PART OF THE LEARNING CURVE...
E.G., SIR ELTON JOHN'S '<u>ELEVATOR MAN</u>' NEVER DID FLY, BUT HIS <u>ROCKET MAN</u> TOOK OFF SOARING AND CARRIED HIM TO THE STARS OF THE FIRMAMENT."

"IF 'THE ENEMY OF CREATIVITY IS GOOD TASTE'—THEN NO WORRIES, AND I'M IN GOOD COMPANY!"

"MORTAL LIFE IS BUT A PRELUDE; DEATH A SEGUE, ETERNITY THE CRESCENDO AND FINAL DESTINATION."

"I'M SICK TO DEATH ABOUT PAYING BIG BUCKS AND LOTS OF THEM, FOR HIGH PRICED BRAND NAME CLOTHES MADE OUTSIDE OF THE U.S.A. IN THIRD WORLD COUNTRIES BY PEOPLE WHO HAVE NO QUALITY CONTROL OR KNOWLEDGE WHATSOEVER OF THE DYNAMIC ANATOMY OF THE HUMAN BODY."

"SOME ARE FOREVER DRAGGING THEIR FEET AND RELUCTANT TO SUBMIT THEIR FINISHED WORK, BECAUSE THEY THINK AND FEEL IRRATIONALLY AND PERHAPS EVEN PERCEIVE SUBCONSCIOUSLY SO, THAT IF AND WHEN THEY DO, THEIR VERY BEST

EFFORT WILL BE REJECTED WHEN "THE BOX" IS OPENED; SCHRÖDINGER'S CAT IS PROVEN TO BE DEAD WITHIN AND THEIR HOPES OF SUCCESS, FAME AND RECOGNITION ARE DASHED. WHEREAS AS LONG AS THEY DON'T SUBMIT THEIR WORK FOR CRITIQUE, THEY CAN TAKE COMFORT IN THE THOUGHT THAT THE CAT IS YET ALIVE AND WELL, THEIR WORK IS PRESTIGIOUS, SAFE AND STRONG, AND THEIR EGO IS STILL INTACT."

"COPY PAPER IS THE FINAL REINCARNATION OF THE RAIN FOREST."

"HUMAN MONSTERS ARE MERELY THE MONSTERS THE TRUE MONSTERS USE AS THEIR ONLY METHOD OF DESTROYING HUMANKIND."

"IF THINKING OUT-SIDE-OF-THE-BOX DOESN'T ACTUALLY GET YOU OUT OF THE BOX ... WHAT'S THE POINT?"

"THE LACK OF IDENTITY IS THE BANE OF MODERN HUMANITY."

"SUCCESS MAKES ME WANT TO SUCCEED MORE."

"I'D LIKE TO SEE MANY THINGS MORE CLEARLY AND NOT JUST WITH MY EYES."

"A MAN CAN SURVIVE AND ENDURE SEPARATION FROM MANY THINGS ... EXCEPT HOPE."

"LIGHT GROWS BRIGHTER AS DARKNESS FALLS,
TO ALL BUT THE BLIND AND THOSE WHO WILL
NOT SEE."

"IF YOU MAKE IT TO THIRTY, YOU CAN MAKE IT TO
FORTY, IF YOU CAN'T ... YOU WON'T."

"IT'S STILL STUNNING TO ME THAT THE LIKES OF
BARACK OBAMA ONCE REDUCED AMERICA INTO A
NATION OF SLOBBERING FAWNING RUBES."

"YOU KNOW I'VE <u>BEEN</u> IN THE MIDDLE OF
NOWHERE, AND IT'S ALL IT'S CRACKED UP TO BE."

"TRUTH IS CONTRARY TO POPULAR BELIEF ...
EVERYONE LIVES FOREVER;
THE ONLY QUESTION IS ...
LOCATION, LOCATION, LOCATION."

"THIS IS A METAPHOR FOR LIFE ITSELF ... DON'T
START AT THE BOTTOM, ALWAYS START AT THE TOP
SHELF, BECAUSE WORKING YOUR WAY UP FROM
THE BOTTOM ONLY GETS YOU TO WHERE YOU
COULD'VE BEEN IN THE FIRST PLACE."

"IT'S INCREDIBLE HOW THE MOUTHS OF SOME CAN
KEEP RUNNING LONG AFTER THEIR BRAIN HAS
STOPPED WORKING."

"THE MOST IMPORTANT MEAL OF THE DAY IS THE
ONE FOR WHICH YOU'RE THANKFUL;
WORK TO EARN AND LEARN TO PAY FOR."

"THE TRAGEDY OF IT ALL IS--THERE ARE TOO MANY PEOPLE IN AMERICA THESE DAYS WHO NEVER GET TIRED OF REACHING FOR NOTHING."

"TERRORISTS HAVEN'T LEARNED ANYTHING AND, THEREFORE, KNOW NOTHING ABOUT LIFE... EXCEPT HOW TO DEFILE IT AND THEN EXTINGUISH IT."

"IF YOU WANT TO GET A JUMP ON THE COMPETITION, MAKE SURE YOU'RE BORN WITH GOOD GENES."

"IF AT FIRST YOU DON'T SUCCEED READ THE INSTRUCTIONS; PREFERABLY IN ENGLISH."

"THE WORLD IS REPLETE WITH PEOPLE THAT BELIEVE IN A PAST THAT NEVER WAS AND REJECT THE TESTIMONY OF THOSE WHO BELIEVE IN THE PAST THAT YET IS."

"THE ONLY PUPPET YOU CAN BELIEVE AND TRUST IS THE ONE WHO'S CUT HIS OWN CORDS."

"I DON'T BELIEVE MY DRIVING IS AGGRESSIVE AND RECKLESS—I SEE IT MORE AS EXPEDIENT AND CREATIVELY FACILITATIVE."

"TOO MANY ARE MERELY ORBITING SANITY TENUOUSLY TETHERED TO THE OUTER LIMITS OF REALITY."

"If as Americans we deserve the leaders we get, then our leaders deserve what's coming to them."

"I love Capuchin monkeys!—Orangutans and frustrated Chimps?... Yah, they'll rip your face off."

"It takes dedicated and creative parenting to raise a child and a village to raise an idiot—and if parents refuse to hone their skills and exercise their responsibility to raise their own children, the village will soon be overrun by idiots."

"Ignorance is no excuse for being ignorant."

"My whole life long I've toed the line ... a serpentine line."

"A man really 'otta stand upright; that's why God made you flat on the bottom."

"The poor in the U.S. of A. ain't got no money, but God bless America ... they've often got everything money can buy."

"There are great days for weddings and birthday parties, but no matter how idyllic, there's never a good day for a funeral."

"EDUCATION ISN'T WORKING IN AMERICA,
SO I GUESS THE DIVERSION OF FOOD AND
ENTERTAINMENT WILL HAVE TO DO."

"'BARRY' BARACK OBAMA, OUR AMBITIOUSLY
(SELF-ADMITTEDLY) LAZY, DISENGAGED
BYSTANDER PRESIDENT TO THE STARS, IS LIKE A
MAN DRIVING A STAGECOACH LOADED WITH
PEOPLE BEING PULLED AT BREAKNECK SPEED BY A
TEAM OF EIGHT TOWARDS A CLIFF, WHILST HIS
HANDPICKED BLIND MAN RIDING SHOTGUN STARES
ON, OUR PRES ALL THE WHILE FIGURING HE'LL
CATCH-UP ON HOW IT ALL TURNED OUT IN THE
POST OR WASHINGTON TIMES OVER HIS MORNING
MARLBORO RED AND COFFEE ... I HAVE NO
RESPECT OR SYMPATHY FOR THE MAN DRIVING THE
COACH, OR HIS CHOICE AT SHOTGUN, ONLY FOR
HIS FRIGHTENED AND CONFUSED PASSENGERS—
AND OF COURSE ... THE HORSES."

"IN HEAVEN WE WON'T BE THE OBJECT OF OUR
OWN AFFECTIONS."

"THE WORDS OF THEIR PROPHETS ARE WRITTEN
BY SOMEONE WHO CAN WRITE—AND NOT SO MUCH
ON THE SUBWAY WALLS ANYMORE, BUT CAN BE
HEARD POURING OUT AND POUNDING IN VULGAR
BASE VIBRATION THROUGH THE TINTED WINDOWS
OF THEIR SLOWLY ROLLING SUVs."

"MY GOALS ARE FOR ME TO KNOW AND FOR YOU
TO NEVER MIND."

"HIS TRUTH IS ALWAYS MARCHING ON, BUT VERY
FEW ARE IN LOCKSTEP WITH IT."

"It's never the right time to do
something wrong."

"Unlike the living, the dead are no longer
at war fighting for scraps of time."

"I've been waiting for this day to come my
whole life long ... finally, <u>slovenly</u> and
<u>raggedy ass sloppy</u> is the new chic."

"Perceived weakness provokes an
aggressive response;
strength projected inspires caution."

"God didn't make me to be a lesser man."

"The pen is mightier than the sword and
often worse—and any ink is bad ink,
especially if it becomes imbedded in
your flesh."

"God's goal is not man's pleasure
but his perfection."

"Mankind has been reduced to dogs fighting
over scraps of time."

"I know guys, friends in fact—that were
told they would never survive outside of
the womb—and you know what ...
they were right."

"YOU KNOW WHAT I'VE NOTICED?
... WHEN BARACK OBAMA PLAYS ROCK PAPER
SCISSORS, IT ALWAYS COMES UP EXECUTIVE
PRIVILEGE."

"ONLY A FOOL OR A COWARD FALLS ON HIS
SWORD BEFORE HE KNOWS IF THE ENEMY HAS
WON THE DAY."

"I MAKE NO APOLOGIES FOR THOSE WHO CAN'T
NAVIGATE THROUGH A SENTENCE
WITHOUT TRIPPING OVER THEIR IGNORANCE."

"I'M BARRY BARACK OBAMA ...
AND LET ME BE ABSOLUTELY AND UNEQUIVOCALLY
TRANSPARENT ... AND THANK YOU."

"THE LORD JESUS CHRIST ENTERED
THE HUMAN RACE NOT AT HIS RECORDED AND
CELEBRATED BIRTH, BUT AT THE MOMENT IN TIME
WHEN ALL OF US ENTER THE HUMAN RACE—
AT HIS RECORDED CONCEPTION."

"BEING LIBERAL IS FINE AND LAUDABLE,
AS LONG AS YOU'RE LIBERAL WITH THAT WHICH
BELONGS TO YOU."

"FOR THOSE OF YOU WHO HAVE A DEATH WISH,
THIS IS A WORLD TEEMING WITH ENDLESS
POSSIBILITIES."

"SOMETIMES GOOD MEN HAVE TO STAND-UP LONG,
BEFORE THEY'RE FREE TO SIT DOWN."

"I WAS TOLD, 'WE DON'T SAY ILLEGAL ALIENS ANYMORE, WE SAY UNDOCUMENTED FUTURE DEMOCRATS.' I SAID, 'WHO'S "WE," SENATOR?' HE SAID, 'WE AMERICANS.' I SAID, 'BULLSHIT!... WAIT A MINUTE, DO "WE AMERICANS" STILL SAY "BULLSHIT?"'"

"THE CONCUSSED AND BESPECTACLED SECRETARY OF STATE HILLARY CLINTON BEING QUESTIONED BEFORE CONGRESS: 'MADAM SECRETARY, TELL US WHAT YOU KNOW ABOUT BENGHAZI.' HILLARY: 'BEN GHAZI, THE CONGRESSIONAL MASSEUR?' ... 'NEVER HEARD OF THE GUY *... AND WHAT DIFFERENCE AT THIS POINT DOES IT MAKE?*'"

"I APPRECIATE HAVING BIRTHDAYS ALMOST AS MUCH AS I APPRECIATE BEING BORN."

"HUMANITY HAS CAST AWAY THE CORDS OF RESTRAINT THAT SECURE US AND ITS ABILITY TO RECOGNIZE AND DISCERN WHAT IS MORALLY RIGHT AND WRONG, GOOD AND EVIL—AND NOW MERELY SEES THINGS IN TERMS OF EITHER DOABLE, OR UNDOABLE."

"THE MONSTERS IN OUR LIVES ARE GOOD AT FRIGHTENING US AND KEEPING US FROM DOING WHAT IS POSSIBLE AND NECESSARY."

"REPUBLICANS AND DEMOCRATS ... YES, THEY'VE GOT A RECIPROCAL RELATIONSHIP LIKE A DOG AND A FIRE HYDRANT"

"THE PRESIDENT BARACK OBAMA ... HE'S NOT SO MUCH A BROTHER-LOVE, AS A DR. FEEL-GOOD."

"RIDING A RICE-BURNING CROTCH ROCKET I'VE BEEN TOLD, IS LIKE TIME SPENT WITH A BONEY ASIAN WHORE: QUICK, UNCOMFORTABLE AND ANNOYINGLY LOUD."

"I'D LIKE TO THINK THAT IF JUDY GARLAND WERE BORN AS A MAN AND A MECHANIC TO BOOT, THAT SHE WOULD'VE NAMED HER ESTABLISHMENT IN KANSAS, *THE JUST FIX IT–FLYING MONKEY WRENCH GARAGE*."

"AMONG OTHERS, THERE WERE <u>THREE THINGS</u> MY FATHER FOUND PARTICULARLY ODIOUS ... A DULL KNIFE, A HAT ON THE KITCHEN TABLE—AND BREAD ON THE GROUND BEING TRODDEN UNDER FOOT."

"HUMANITY BEWARE, FOR GOD IS THE ABSOLUTE AND ULTIMATE TERRORIST TO ALL THOSE WHO REFUSE HIS LOVING KINDNESS AND GENTLE PERSUASION, AND IN LIEU, NEGLECT SO GREAT SALVATION."

"JUST A WORD TO THE WISE FROM GUNSLINGERS, TRAPEZE ARTISTS AND CRACK ADDICTS ... 'MAKE <u>DAMN SURE</u> IT'S THERE WHEN YOU REACH FOR IT!'"

<u>"HEROES ARE GIVEN CROWNS AND WINGS, THE REST OF US ARE GIVEN HEROES AND (RED BULL)."</u>

"YOU'RE ONLY AS CRAZY AS YOU <u>ACT</u> AND AS DUMB AS YOU <u>THINK</u>."

"I'M NOT A FAN OF ABORTION BECAUSE I'M NO FAN OF MURDER, BUT OH … 'IT'S NOT MURDER!' YOU SAY … WELL … PERHAPS YOU'LL HAVE THE OPPORTUNITY TO EXPLAIN THAT THEORY TO <u>THE AUTHOR OF LIFE</u> ON JUDGMENT DAY."

"UNLESS WE CAN FIGURE OUT A WAY TO TURN WATER INTO GASOLINE, INVENT AN ANTIGRAVITY MACHINE AND PERFECT THE HOVERCRAFT AND TRANSPORTER, THE CHINESE AND ARABS OWN … 'AMERICA THE ~~BEAUTIFUL~~ BORROWER.'"

"WHEN YOU START TO NOTICE THAT THE ENGAGEMENT RING IS SERIOUSLY MORE PRECIOUS AND BEAUTIFUL THAN THE ONE ON WHOSE FINGER IT RESIDES … YOU'VE GOT A BIG PROBLEM HOME SKILLET."

"AS A WRITER OF THOUGHTS, QUOTES AND OBSERVATIONS, I'M AMAZED AT HOW MUCH HASN'T YET BEEN SAID."

"DUDE THAT'S NOT A BUMP ON YOUR HEAD, I JUST THINK ALL THE REST OF YOUR HEAD HAS CAVED IN AROUND IT."

"WHEN THE SCREW TURNS AND TIGHTENS DOWN ON THE TOPIC OF ABORTION AND <u>ABORTION ON DEMAND</u> IN PARTICULAR, IT MAY BE DEBATABLE AS TO WHO THE MURDERER IS AND WHICH THE ACCOMPLICE IS, BUT THERE IS ABSOLUTELY AND UNEQUIVOCALLY NO DOUBT AS TO <u>WHOM THE VICTIM IS</u>."

"REGARDING WARFARE, HUMANITY CAN'T WIN AGAINST ITSELF; ONLY GOD CAN DEFEAT MAN."

"Genius isn't building a better mousetrap,
it's engineering a mouse that can't be
caught."

"The decedents of slaves see things
differently than the decedents of free
men—and as long as they do, they may never
be free."

"The hallmark of an obedient Christian is
having a long fuse and a ledger of short
accounts."

"The tyranny of liberty without limits leads
to decadence and anarchy."

"If you coddle a rebellious jackass long
enough, you'll create a monster."

"Really? ... I mean freakin' really!—
the Moslems don't need weapons to follow
Islam ... do they?"

"For better or for worse, we've all had a
hand in making our lives, America and this
world what it is today; for some of us, more
of a hand than others."

"Most merely retire from;
the wise retire to."

"OH, THE TERRORISTS WILL ANSWER TO A HIGHER AUTHORITY ALL RIGHT—AND IT'S NOT GOING TO BE ALLAH."

"EVEN IN A SLOPPY AND DISGRACEFUL BATTLE SOMEONE HAS TO WIN."

"I'M A WRITER, AND I KNOW UNEQUIVOCALLY THAT HARPER LEE HAD NO SISTER NAMED GINGER."

"PEOPLE WHO ARE HOPING TO BE ELECTED TO HIGH POLITICAL OFFICE ARE CALLED … A. (CANDIDATES) B. (KENNEDYS) C. (BUSHES AND CLINTONS) D. (ALL OF THE ABOVE)"

"I DON'T KNOW IF IT'S A GUY THING OR JUST A ME THING, BUT I DON'T JUST WANT TO KNOW THAT SOMETHING WORKS, I WANT TO KNOW HOW IT WORKS, AND WHEN IT DOESN'T WORK, I WANT TO KNOW WHY IT DOESN'T WORK, AND IF IT DOESN'T WORK, I WANT TO FIX IT AND MAKE IT WORK; ALTHOUGH, INTERESTINGLY ENOUGH, POLITICIANS IN GENERAL AND CONGRESS AND THE SENATE IN PARTICULAR HAVE NEVER SUFFERED FROM SUCH A MALADY."

"MOST CAN'T PARLAY SHIT FOR BRAINS AND WHISKY FOR GUTS INTO A TIME-HONORED WINNING COMBINATION."

"I'M RATHER DISAPPOINTED TO FIND OUT THAT ITCHY AND BURNEY ARE MERELY HEMORRHOID SYMPTOMS AND NOT LOVEABLE SESAME STREET CHARACTERS."

"I'D PREFER TO HAVE THE QUESTION POSED ...
'HOW'D YOU GET HEALED BRO!'
RATHER THAN, 'WHERE'D YOU GET THE COOL
CANE DUDE?'"

"INCONGRUITY: A QUADRIPLEGIC ISIS MIME
SHRIEKING IN A WHEELCHAIR QUARANTINED
BEHIND THE THICK TEMPERED OPAQUE GLASS OF A
SOUND-PROOF CUBIC ISOLATION CHAMBER ON
DISPLAY AT THE LOUVRE IN PARIS."

"MANY OF AMERICA'S WOES ARE DUE TO *THE
FACT* THAT TOO MANY OF HER CITIZENS DON'T
HAVE ANY SKIN IN THE GAME—AND THE RIGHT TO
VOTE THAT ENSURES THEY NEVER WILL."

"BLOOD STILL CRIES-OUT, FOR GOD NOT ONLY
FEARFULLY AND WONDERFULLY ENGINEERED THE
MARVEL AND BEGUILING PROPERTIES OF HUMAN
BLOOD, HE ENGINEERED THE RELENTLESS TRAIL
AND DOGGED STAIN OF ETERNAL DIRECTIONALITY
TO THE VERY HANDS THAT SHED IT."

"NO ONE HAS TO AGREE UPON THE TRUTH FOR IT
TO BE SO; ONLY LIES NEED A CONSENSUS."

"AS CHRISTIANS WE DON'T MERELY HAVE TIME ON
OUR SIDE, WE HAVE ETERNITY."

"THE THING THAT KEEPS YOU ALIVE AND WELL ARE
YOUR BRAINS NOT YOUR BULLETS."

"THE MISTAKE MEN MAKE IN MARRYING THAT
LEADS TO DIVORCE IS NOT THAT THEY SAY AT

TIMES TO THE RIGHT WOMEN NO, BUT THAT THEY SAY TO THE WRONG WOMEN YES."

"NO MERCHANT HAS EVER WANTED A SATISFIED CUSTOMER; THEY WANT CUSTOMERS THAT ARE HUNGRY AND CONSTANTLY CRAVING."

"ALL THAT IS NECESSARY FOR THE TRIUMPH OF EVIL IS THAT ~~GOOD MEN~~ GOD DO NOTHING."

"OH, SIN WILL BE JUDGED, BUT NEITHER BY MOHAMED OR HIS GOD, NOR BY HIS DEVOTEES, FOLLOWERS AND THOSE ENAMORED OF HIM, BUT BY THE VERY SON OF THE GOD OF ABRAHAM, ISAAC AND JACOB."

"MAYBE GOD ONLY KNOWS WHEN LIFE BEGINS, BUT I KNOW WHEN IT ENDS; WHEN YOU MAKE IT IMPOSSIBLE FOR IT TO CONTINUE."

"SOME THIRTY YEARS AGO I WORKED IN A HIGH SCHOOL AS A CUSTODIAN AND WAS GIVEN A RING OF KEYS THAT CONTAINED A VERY THIN ORIGINAL KEY REFERRED TO AS <u>THE OLD MASTER</u>—AND WHEN I RETURNED THIRTY YEARS LATER AS THE SCHOOL'S ENGINEER, SURPRISINGLY THE KEY WAS STILL IN SERVICE, HOWEVER, DUE TO POLITICAL CORRECTNESS AND RACIAL SENSITIVITY, THE KEY IS NOW REFERRED TO AS—
<u>THE ELDERLY WHITE RACIST</u>."

"THEY DON'T ALWAYS DANCE ON YOUR GRAVE WHEN YOU FAIL, ONLY WHEN YOU SUCCEED IN DEFEATING THEM, THEREFORE, I WOULD RATHER WITH NO REGRETS BOLDLY LIVE A LIFE WORTHY OF MY ENEMIES REJOICING AT MY DEATH, THEN

SAFELY PERISH IN WELL-DESERVED AND
CAREFULLY CULTIVATED PEACEFULLY OBSCURE
ANONYMITY."

I'VE COME TO THE CONCLUSION THAT MY LIFE HAS
ALWAYS BEEN A LIFE WORTH RISKING—
AND THEIRS ARE LIVES WORTH SAVING."

"THE WICKED AND BASE DO NOT RECOGNIZE GOOD
WHEN THEY SEE IT OR EVIL WHEN THEY DO IT."

"KIDS ARE SMARTER THAN YOU THINK,
BUT NOT AS SMART AS THEY THINK."

"GOOGLE SEARCH OF THE ETERNALLY HOPEFUL ...
QUESTION: 'ARE EXTRA THICK, BONELESS
COUNTRY STYLE PORK CHOPS HIGH IN
ANTIOXIDANTS?'"

"YOU CAN QUENCH THE LOVE OF GOD AS EASILY
AS YOU CAN FREEZE FIRE."

"WHEN YOU'RE LOOKING FOR A GOOD WOMAN IN
TEMPERAMENT, PERSONALITY AND PHYSICAL
ATTRACTIVENESS YOU'LL BE WANTING SOFT
CONTOURS; IN GODLINESS AND CHARACTER,
SHARP ANGLES."

"SAFETY FIRST YES, BUT ...
'A .357 MAGNUM COLT PYTHON WITH A SIX-INCH
BARREL TRIGGER-LOCKED AND PADLOCKED IN A
STRONGBOX OUT OF THE REACH OF CHILDREN
WITH ITS HOLLOW-POINT BULLETS IN A SEPARATE
AND UNDISCLOSED LOCATION IS NOT A QUICK-

DRAW SELF-DEFENSE GIMMICK ENDORSED BY THE N.R.A.'"

"IT'S CURIOUS TO ME THAT MATHEMATICALLY THIS TWENTY-FIRST CENTURY, THAT IS TO SAY, CENTURY *TWENTY-ONE,* IS THREE TIMES SEVEN; SEVEN BEING THE NUMBER OF PERFECTION IN THEOLOGY, I.E. COMPLETION, WHICH ALWAYS REFERS TO GOD ... THE NUMBER THREE ALSO REFERRING TO THE TRIUNE GOD; I.E., GOD THE FATHER, GOD THE SON AND GOD THE HOLY SPIRIT ... INTERESTING ... NAY?"

"REST IS BEST ACCOMPLISHED WHEN YOU'RE TIRED; FORGIVENESS WHEN YOU'RE GUILTY."

"YOU DON'T HAVE TO WORRY ABOUT SOME PEOPLE GOING CRAZY, BECAUSE THEY'RE ALREADY THERE."

"OUR LOT HAS BECOME A HOUSE OF CARDS IN A GAME GOD IS LETTING US PLAY."

"REMEMBER, IF ANYTHING CAN GO WRONG IT WILL, BECAUSE THERE'S ALWAYS A FLY IN THE OINTMENT OF THE SILVER LINING IN EVERY CLOUD THAT'S PASSING YOU BY."

"SOMETIMES THE *CHEF'S CHOICE* ISN'T ON THE MENU, BECAUSE IT'S THE RESTAURANT DOWN THE STREET."

"How intelligent can you be if you can't prove it?"

"Sometimes you have to do something drastic to stop something horrific."

"If you're going to lose yourself in thought, let it be creative thought."

"At times what men afford you by God's design is the opportunity to help them."

"Well dude, if you had wings you should've been flying."

"Alcohol does nothing to enhance your beauty; only the beauty of others."

"Your enemy is anyone trying to kill you; motives notwithstanding."

"The small hide behind the courageous and benevolent big; the cowardly and contemptible behind the masses."

"Like my old Granddaddy once said to me ... 'Son, if you take your girlfriend or wife out to dinner someday to a fine seafood restaurant—and while perusing the menu she says she'd like to have crab legs and a lobster tail, NEVER POINT IT OUT TO HER AND SAY ... 'But Darlin', you already have crab legs and a lobster tail.'"

"Chopsticks like swords will always
cross when they're not even."

"There is no Liberal or Conservative
Christians, only obedient
and disobedient ones."

"The only good thing about war humanity
has been denied is its end."

"Like so many things in life; so many people
like the finest of tea leaves, have only so
much to give—and once they've given their
all ... they're considered expendable
trash."

"The soul of a victim tends towards
festering; the spirit of a victor
embraces healing."

"Only God knows what I would've been like
if it weren't for sin in my life; not only my
sin, but the aggregate of the thousands of
years of generations that chose sin before
me."

"The answer is not more money, because
even the obscenely and idle rich still wrap
their lips around revolvers and powerful
prescription drugs attempting to escape
the vanity of their manifestly tenuous lot."

"What good is having a God that *doesn't*
or *can't* answer?"

"FEAR NOT, TABASCO© IS OUR FRIEND—
AND I KNOW, BECAUSE I'VE ASKED."

"GOD IS ALL FOR SIMPLICITY AND THE ULTIMATE
PRAGMATIST, THEREFORE, THE GREAT PROBLEM
FOR HUMANITY IS NOT FINDING SALVATION ...
BUT ACCEPTING IT."

"ONE THING I KNOW FOR SURE ABOUT INVESTING;
WHEN THE STOCK MARKET GOES UP ...
THE GAMBLERS ARE HAPPY."

"WHEN IT COMES TO ALL AMERICANS BEING ALL-
COMPASSIONATE, TO ALL COMERS, UNDER ALL
CIRCUMSTANCES, AT ALL TIMES AND AT ALL COST
... MAYBE, JUST MAYBE, IT'S BETTER NOT TO RISK
KILLING THE *ONLY* GOOSE THAT KNOWS HOW TO
KEEP LAYING THE GOLDEN EGGS."

"THE QUESTION IS ASKED 'IS IT SAFE?'—
AND THE ANSWER IS, THERE'S NO SAFE PLACE
ON THIS EARTH, ONLY PLACES LESS DANGEROUS
THAN OTHERS."

"I DON'T ALWAYS BELIEVE WHAT I READ,
BUT I ALWAYS BELIEVE IN WHAT I WRITE."

"A HEADS-UP FROM THE MASTER TO THE
NEOPHYTES; ALWAYS KEEP THE TIP OF YOUR
CHOPSTICKS EVEN."

"I PULLED UP BESIDE *THE LAW* ...
AND *THE LAW* MADE ME WONDER."

"Don't concern yourself, because it was me alone talking—but it was the Bourbon that loosened my tongue."

"No one wins by quitting; winners run harder to overtake those that have passed them by, as well as to keep those in pursuit from running them into the ground."

"A stupid reckless man spends his lifetime hitting his head because he's oblivious to the ubiquitous obstacles surrounding him—and an arrogant man is forever ducking, even when there's absolutely no chance of hitting his head on aught but a jagged piece of sky."

"As regards culpability and vindication; God knew what He was doing when He invented the constitution and indelible stain of blood."

"I would rather be exalted than have someone else diminished and brought low."

"My neighborhood hasn't really changed all that much since I was a kid; except of course for the skin color, caliber and clip capacity of the gangsters, punks and thugs."

"It's marvelous to me that God Himself, who created us and watched us fall, paid for our lavish sin with His own precious Blood on the brutal cross at Calvary."

"If one is afforded liberty and a chance for equality with all <u>others</u> and does not embrace and run free with it, the onus of the consequences thereof is upon them … and not upon the <u>others</u>."

"If you're a drunk you're no longer calling the shots, <u>the shots</u> are calling you."

"A Canadian 'facial' is when your friend surreptitiously shakes up your ice-cold pounder of Labatt's Blue before you open it."

"Oh please tell me; on who's part is it racist, to consider that somebody who is half black and half white … *is black*?"

"The waistline of a good pair of pants will always let you know when it's time to lose weight—Spandex™ … not so much."

"A man's life is only as precious as the lives of those he's willing to risk it for to save."

"A cross around the neck is but a symbol of salvation; Jesus in your heart is the proof that justifies wearing it."

"Radical Moslems faithful to the Quran and the Hadith do not want Western liberties for Islam; they want the West for Islam."

"IF AMERICA CONTINUES HER CURRENT TACK OF SPREADING HER LEGS WIDE FOR THE WORLD AT LARGE, WHAT CAN WE REASONABLY EXPECT BUT A NATION FULL OF IGNOBLE AND ARROGANT, INGLORIOUS BASTARDS?"

"THE KRYPTONITE OF MERE MORTALS IS EXHAUSTIBLE, BUT COURTESY OF THE KING OF GLORY, THE DELIVERANCE OF WE WHO ARE WILLING, IS ABSOLUTE."

"IN THE WORLD OF THE ANCIENT ROMANS, TO APPEASE AND CALM THE DESPERATELY RESTLESS MASSES, THEY INVENTED THE TOOL AND CONCEPT OF BREAD AND CIRCUS, I.E., FOOD AND ENTERTAINMENT—AND WE IN THE MODERN AND FAR MORE DECADENT WESTERN WORLD, HAVE DONE THEM ONE BETTER VIA THE FOOD NETWORK; <u>WE'VE TURNED FOOD ... INTO ENTERTAINMENT</u>."

"IT IS UNDERSTOOD THAT ... "MEN ARE STIMULATED BY SIGHT."—SO WHEN IT COMES TO THE TOTAL VEILING OF WOMEN IN ISLAM; SOMEONE TELL ME HOW YOU COULD BE PHYSICALLY DESIROUS OF, AND ROMANTICALLY ATTRACTED TO ... SOMEONE YOU CANNOT, NOR HAVE EVER SEEN?"

"IN THE GRAND THOUGH NOT ULTIMATE SCHEME OF THINGS, LIFE ITSELF IS A DEATH SENTENCE."

"THOUGH IT MAY BE AN AMERICAN CLICHÉ OR NO, YOU'VE STILL GOT TO LISTEN TO THE OLD STOIC INDIAN—EVEN IF HE DOESN'T SPEAK."

"FRET NOT, FOR PURE EVIL <u>HAS TO AND WILL BE</u>
ANSWERED WITH HOLY FIRE."

"IN ANY GIVEN INSTANCE, IF THE PROPER
PUNCTUATION HOBBLES THE EXPRESSION AT
HAND, THEN ONE MUST USE IMPROPER
PUNCTUATION TO MORE PERFECTLY EXPRESS
A FREE FLOW OF THE CREATIVE THOUGHT."

"ALL OF MY LIFE IS A QUOTE; SOME RECORDED,
SOME NOT ... AND SO IS YOURS."

"QUITE APPARENTLY TO ME, WHEN IT COMES TO
DARK GLOBAL BANKING AND DEALINGS WITH
THIEVING WORLD WAR TWO NAZIS AND THEIR
MODERN BUT EQUIVALENT ILK; MUCH LIKE LAS
VEGAS, WHAT HAPPENS IN ZURICH SWITZERLAND,
STAYS IN ZURICH SWITZERLAND."

"TAKE MY WORD FOR IT; IN MY NEIGHBORHOOD ON
THE LOWER EAST SIDE, THE ECHOING RASPY
TOOTHLESS CACKLE OF A WRETCHED CHAIN-
SMOKING DRUNKEN WHORE BEING WAFTED ALOFT
ON A WARM SUMMER NIGHT'S BREEZE ...
IS UNMISTAKABLE."

"JACKASSES DON'T HAVE UNIQUE AND CREATIVE
STYLE ... THEY HAVE FLASHY ANTICS."

"THESE DAYS IN AMERICA THE POWERS THAT BE
ARE GIVING FOLKS ONLY ONE STONE
AND TOO MANY BIRDS TO KILL."

"Sometimes you just have to ask the question; 'what's wrong with that dude; did he sprinkle too much *schizophren* on his corn flakes at breakfast again?'"

"One of the greatest and glaring secrets of America is ... we still think we are."

"Sometimes you really have to get into it, before you can get out from under it."

"It's always good to have a life other than the one you're currently occupied in."

"It's not sweetening the deal to know that your girlfriend is becoming a Goth, but only one fingernail at a time."

"A man isn't protected and delivered by the symbols of power; he's saved by *the power* behind the symbols."

"In my experience, if you don't put your own stink and spin on your life... somebody else will."

"Yah I've got a stress ball ... and it's loaded with Xanax®."

"One of the greatest problems for modern America is—we suffer insufferable fools gladly."

"I THINK IT'S VERY SIGNIFICANT THAT
CHRISTIANITY IS A RELATIONSHIP AND NOT
AN *ISM*."

"IF GOD LET EVERYONE GO TO HEAVEN; IT
WOULDN'T PROVE THAT HE'S LOVING,
IT WOULD DISPROVE THAT HE'S HOLY."

"A CAR FOLLOWING YOU AT NIGHT WITH A
HEADLIGHT OUT, LIKE A ONE-EYED MAN,
ALWAYS MAKES YOU A LITTLE BIT NERVOUS."

"I'M ONLY MAKING IT UP IF IT TURNS OUT
NOT TO BE TRUE."

"I MUCH PREFER TAKING SHOWERS TO BATHS,
BECAUSE I LIKE TO WASH THE FILTH CLEAN OFF OF
ME—AND SEEM TO HAVE AN INNATE AND PRIMAL
AVERSION TO STEWING IN MY OWN RICH JUICES."

"MAKING KILLING MORE EFFICIENT DOESN'T MAKE
WAR LESS LIKELY."

"A METHOD TO THE MADNESS DOESN'T JUSTIFY
THE MADNESS, OR FOR THAT MATTER ...
THE METHOD."

"FEW PEOPLE ARE SMART ENOUGH TO KNOW
WHEN TO ACT STUPID; THE STUPID HOWEVER,
SUFFER FROM NO SUCH AFFLICTION."

"THERE'S NO EXPIRATION DATE ON MURDER AND
IN GOD'S ECONOMY <u>NONE AT ALL ON ANY SIN</u>;

UNTIL BY HIM, LIKE ALL SIN THAT'S REPENTED OF,
IS <u>BY GRACE ALONE</u> FREELY FORGIVEN."

"ONCE PANINI SANDWICHES FOR ME WERE
MERELY THEORETICAL; NOW THANKS TO THE
GEORGE FOREMAN GRILL I INHERITED FROM MY
MOM, I'VE FOUND THEM TO BE AN ABSOLUTELY
DELICIOUS AND CREATIVE MEDIUM QUITE
ESSENTIAL TO MY GASTRONOMIC REPERTOIRE."

"NEVER WORRY OR WONDER WHY THOSE
NOW DEAD WANTED TO KILL YOU ...
BECAUSE THEY'RE DEAD."

"THOSE WHO OPERATE MILITARY KILLER DRONES
HAVE BECOME THE COLLATERALLY CHALLENGED,
CASUAL EXTINGUISHERS OF HUMAN LIFE."

"HUMAN NATURE CANNOT BE SUBDUED BUT
ONLY SUBJECTED."

"WE'RE BEING REDUCED TO A BRUTAL RACE WITH
FLASHES OF HUMANITY."

"YOU CAN'T LEGISLATE MORALITY BECAUSE
HUMAN NATURE IS NONNEGOTIABLE."

"I'VE COME TO FIND THAT THE MORE TENUOUS
THEIR LOT, THE THINNER THEIR SKIN."

"ONCE A CHRISTIAN FOREVER A CHRISTIAN—AND
IF YOU'RE 'NO LONGER A CHRISTIAN' ...
YOU NEVER ONCE WERE."

"THE ONLY THING THE COLD HAS EVER DONE
FOR ME IS AFFORD ME THE OPPORTUNITY TO
FREEZE IN IT."

"NO MATTER HOW FEEBLE OUR EFFORT, PRAYER IS
THE ONLY COMMUNICATION THAT'S <u>ALWAYS</u>
RECIPROCAL AND <u>NEVER</u> MISUNDERSTOOD."

"HOW DO I DO IT YOU ASK? ...
I DO IT BY OBSERVING, ABSORBING, PROCESSING
AND EXTRUDING...HOW DO YOU DO IT?"

"JESUS THE <u>GREAT PHYSICIAN</u> WOULD AGREE,
THAT THE MOTTO OF THE MEDICAL PROFESSION
SHOULD BE THE MOTTO FOR WE CHRISTIANS AND
CHRISTIANITY ... 'PRIMUM NON NOCERE' ...
'<u>FIRST DO NO HARM</u>.'"

"NO TRUE JOY COMES WITHOUT CHALLENGE; THE
CHALLENGING JOYS ARE RICH AND COME DEAR."

"I LIMIT MYSELF TO THREE DRINKS A DAY;
BEER, WINE AND <u>GOOD</u> SCOTCH."

"'CHALLENGED AND ENGAGED? ... I THINK NOT!'
BECAUSE THE ORDER OF THE NEW DAY IS—
'STROKE ME, STROKE ME ...
I WANT TO BE APPEASED BY YOU.'"

"I HEARD CLEARLY EVERY WORD MY FINANCIAL
ADVISOR SAID AND ONLY UNDERSTOOD THREE OF
THEM ... 'LOTS OF MONEY...'"

"IF YOU FIND YOURSELF REPEATEDLY SPELLING FUN, 'PHUN' ... YOU'RE PROBABLY IN DIRE NEED OF A LONG VACATION."

"DUDE, IF YOU CAN'T STAND THE HEAT, YOU'LL BE WANTING TO STAY OUT-A-HELL A WHOLE LOT MORE THAN YOUR MAMA'S KITCHEN."

"YOU HAVE TO ENJOY THE BEAUTY YOU FIND, BECAUSE YOU CAN'T ALWAYS CREATE THE BEAUTY YOU SEEK."

"AFTER HIS OWN IMAGE, GOD DELIBERATELY MADE THE WILL OF MAN STRONG—AND ONLY THE LIVING GOD CAN WIN BACK THE COVETED PRIZE AND CRACK THE TOUGH AND WAYWARD NUT OF HUMANITY."

"OUR HEROES ARE ONLY ONE OF US ... UNTIL THEY BECOME HEROES."

"OH JESUS HAD SKIN IN THE GAME ALL RIGHT; HIS VERY OWN FLESH AND BLOOD—AND ONLY GOD THE FATHER KNOWS HOW FANTASTICALLY AND INFINITELY MUCH MORE."

"AMERICANS HAVE FAILED AT LEADING, CONTROLLING AND INFLUENCING THE WORLD FOR GOOD, BECAUSE WE NO LONGER VALUE OR EVALUATE THINGS WITH A JUDEO-CHRISTIAN PERSPECTIVE AND THE CLEAR EYES OF OUR WISE FOUNDING FATHERS—AND NOW SEE THINGS MERELY THROUGH THE SKEWED PRISMS PROVIDED FOR US BY—WASHINGTON AND WALL STREET, HOLLYWOOD AND THE A.C.L.U."

"Thomas Jefferson or Bob Marley; we all create the reality in which we want to live."

"Who among us but our Cardiologist *doesn't* know—that not enough salt, means not enough flavor."

"Of all the gifts I give, I'm exceedingly pleased and quite certain the receivers prefer *THE GIVER* ... to his gifts."

"'Bottom feeders' are what they are and do what they must; however, in their defense, they do manage to avoid feeding among the upper crust of society and getting nourished in the rich and thick oil slicks and inevitably treacherous infinite tangle of excruciating human flotsam."

"Not all of us can ignore what's hanging over our heads so that we might focus on that which is right before our eyes."

"How I envy the soaring birds of prey, for how quickly and cleanly they can rise to ride the thermals above the battle of men and escape the deluge and destruction when the fire, tsunami, volcano or earthquake comes; would that moral, earthbound, mortal man, by the same grace and design, be lofted beyond the reach of the coming fire of ... *'THE PERFECT STORM.'*"

"As representative and observer of the world at large let me say; Americans like any other people and America like any and

ALL OTHER NATIONS—*THOROUGHLY DESERVES* THE
CONSEQUENCES OF WHATSOEVER WE SANCTION
AND ARE WILLING TO TOLERATE."

"IN AMERICA ON THE SO-CALLED *BLACK FRIDAY*
AFTER THANKSGIVING EVERYONE BUYS WHAT
THEY DON'T REALLY NEED; ON *GOOD FRIDAY*
DURING PASSOVER JUST OUTSIDE OF JERUSALEM
TWO THOUSAND YEARS AGO, ALL OF US FREELY
RECEIVED WHAT WE COULD NEVER AFFORD."

"IT'S GOT TO BE NORAH JONES—
BECAUSE I'M STARTING TO GET SLEEPY."

"I DON'T WANT ANYTHING I'M GOING TO HAVE TO
WAIT FOR SOMEBODY TO DIE TO GET."

"SOMEONE OUGHT TO DO BARACK THE PRESIDENT
OBAMA A SOLID AND TELL HIM THAT IF THE
STRONG, AND IN FACT ONLY SUIT HE WEARS IS THE
CHARISMATIC ONE; IT'S STILL GOING TO GET VERY
BADLY SOILED WHEN HE EVENTUALLY AND
INEVITABLY GETS KICKED TO THE CURB ASSHOLE
OVER TIN CUP WITH HIS PEN AND CELL
PHONE IN HAND."

"A MONSTER IS JUST ONE OF US—AND OFTEN
TIMES, A BONA-FIDE HERO WHO STUMBLES AND
FALLS—AND ALL OF US DEARLY LOVE TO DESTROY
... OUR MONSTERS."

"THE POWERS THAT BE ARE GLEEFULLY TOUTING
'OUR' SAVING OF MILLIONS, WHILE THEY'RE
LAVISHLY THROWING AWAY OUR HARD-WON
TRILLIONS."

"A COMPUTER VIRUS IS LIKE THE ALIEN IN
RIPLEY'S SPACECRAFT ON HER TRIP BACK HOME
TO EARTH ... 'ARE WE THERE YET!'"

"IT'S STUNNING TO ME, THAT THE PRISTINE FLESH
OF SIMPLE HUMANITY IS AS UNABLE TO RESIST THE
TATTOOIST'S STINGING PEN AND STAINING INK, AS
THE CRISP AND FRESH COTTON CANVAS WAS TO
RESIST THE PAINT AND STROKES OF THE
MASTERS."

"'EVERYTHING'S GOING TO HELL' THEY DECLARE
BLITHELY—AND THEY'RE RIGHT,
BECAUSE EVERYONE'S RUNNING AWAY FROM
KEEPING IT ALL FROM GOING TO HELL."

"DO YOU WANT TO KNOW WHAT SURPRISINGLY
ADVANTAGEOUS THING MY JOB HAS TAUGHT ME TO
DO? ... ADAPT AND MITIGATE INCOMPETENCE."

"REGARDING THE *SWINE FLU* OUTBREAK AND
PANIC OF "2009," MY TAKE ON THE WHOLE THING
IS—THAT 'CLEANLINESS, IS NEXT TO ...
IMPOSSIBLE.'"

"I'M A BIT OF A SPARTAN MINIMALIST, IF THAT'S
NOT REDUNDANT, BECAUSE I DON'T LIKE CLUTTER
AND TOO MUCH STUFF IN MY HOUSE; I LIKE THE
WIDE OPEN SPACES; I LIKE BEING ABLE TO MOVE
FREELY FROM ROOM TO ROOM WITHOUT HAVING TO
NAVIGATE—AND I LIKE THE IDEA OF BEING ABLE TO
SWING A DEAD CAT, EVEN A BIG ONE, WITHOUT
KNOCKING A THING TO THE FLOOR."

"Even the wise and venerable Emperor at the table will look like an incompetent fool if he's provided with a pair of crooked chopsticks."

"I often talk too loud in private conversations because I want everyone to overhear what I have to say."

"My friend; I'm fallen, you're fallen, we're all broken and fallen— and the tragedy of it is, that we-all-of-us are too comfortable in our brokenness and fallenness—and the advantage I have over you right now is, I know we're all fallen— and I know the way out of It ... *for us all.*"

"I may think I'm that smart, but believe me, in moments of lucidity I know I'm not, but I am smart enough to give you the heads-up and let you know ... that I'm not all that smart."

"No matter where you go—'People are people' they say comfortingly—and I quite agree; which is why God has us tethered here and will never let us permanently off of this planet.—My condolences to N.A.S.A."

"Collectively we're all screwed, individually however, there's still hope."

"Feel free to forsake hubris, for it stands a fool's errand."

"I WAS TAUGHT THIS BY MY MOTHER FROM A
YOUNG AND TENDER AGE; ALWAYS KEEP THEM
SEPARATE, WHITES WITH WHITES, AND COLORED
WITH COLORED ... CLOTHES THAT IS ...
WHAT DID YOU THINK I WAS REFERRING TO?"

"IF YOU THINK IT'S A FANTASTIC LOOKING LIFELIKE
GARDEN GNOME, THINK TWICE BEFORE YOU BEND
DOWN CLOSER TO GIVE IT A LOOK-SEE ...
I WISH I HAD."

"WE ALL WANT TO BE LIKE OUR HEROES, BECAUSE
WE THINK OUR HEROES ARE IMMUNE TO FEAR AND
PAIN ... THEY'RE NOT ... FOR THE MOST PART,
THEY'RE JUST LIKE US—*ONLY WILLING*."

"DURING THE THREE YEARS OF HIS EARTHLY
MINISTRY; JESUS WAS ON *THE ULTIMATE ...
WALKABOUT*."

"DURING BOW HUNTING SEASON, I ALWAYS HAVE
MY DEER AND ELK BUTCHERED AND THE MEAT
PROCESSED WAY BACK IN THE DEEP WOODS AT A
PLACE CALLED *TWO GUYS AND A KNIFE* ...
FORMERLY KNOWN AS THE NOW DEFUNCT
SURGICAL PRACTICE OF—*TWO SURGEONS AND
A SCALPEL*."

"SHE WAS NOT BLIND FROM BIRTH BUT
ALL SEEING, UNTIL WE STARTED THROWING
BROKEN GLASS INTO THE BRILLIANTLY CLEAR
EYES OF JUSTICE."

"MUCH OF LIFE IS MUCK, AND WE ARE BUT THE
FAITHFUL TRAVELING THROUGH IT."

"Could <u>the cold hand</u> be that of God at times, which drives us to the warmth of the redeeming and healing fire?"

"In many cases psychoanalysis and psychotherapeutic head shrinking doesn't work for the same reason one of the cardinal rules of locksmithing exists, namely—though a very difficult lock can be picked, *you can't pick a lock that's broken.*"

"You know what, I think I'm going to borrow this, do you think the universe will mind?"

"All those that have hurt me deserve to be in shackles and in chains—and indeed they are, however, they're shackled and chained to me—and I'm the only one that holds the key."

"The would-be liberal justifiers defensively plead their cause and say: "They're not guilty of these atrocities, they're just *disturbed*"—and indeed they are, though the template we keep trying to skirt stands firm and clear; hell will be a very disturbing place—full of people perfectly *disturbed.*"

"Many of those who invest in gold as a hedge and forsake and loathe paper money think that when calamity comes and judgment finally falls, they'll be the only ones to survive and remain standing ... and they will indeed, until those with only *folding* money, empty stomachs and loaded guns find them."

"Bear with me, because I'm trying to solve
a literary problem; namely …
getting published."

"Forget that arm twisted out of its socket;
I'd be more concerned about this skin
crawlingly sharp boning knife blade
dancing over your carotid artery right
about now if I were you."

"In the dire straits of a survival situation,
one must always err on the side of doing
more, than less."

"I believe during his eight years in office,
President George W. Bush was snookered,
slickered, bamboozled and hornswoggled
by all the shiny objects in The White House
and just lost it in the sun—
and in Barack Hussein's administration …
Obama is the Sun."

"Yah man, I know she'd be attractive if she
lost some weight, but dude, you can't lose
that much ugly and survive."

"The reason America is now stumbling badly
and grievously languishing globally, is
because *America the truly unique*, is quickly
abdicating herself to *America the common*—
for we have, for far too long now, been
systematically exchanging and
compromising the wealth and true source
of our liberty and greatness for mere
license, thus weakening us all—and rather
than diligently dragging the rest of the
feeble-willed world kicking and screaming

INTO THE LIGHT OF A NEW DAY, WE'RE COMFORTABLY SETTLING ON OUR LEES AND SINKING WITH THEM INTO THE ENCROACHING, HOMOGENEOUS PAST DARKNESS AND FINAL COUNTDOWN TO OUR COLLECTIVE ULTIMATE OBLIVION."

"DEATH AND EVERYTHING THAT PRECEDES IT, INCLUDING THE CROSS OF 'SO GREAT SALVATION' IS THE RESULT OF REBELLION AND HUMAN SIN."

"TO RECOUP MY LOSSES ON THE NASDAQ, I'M WAITING FOR A BLOOD PRESSURE MEDICATION TO BE DEVELOPED AND THEN QUICKLY APPROVED BY THE FDA THAT I CAN HEAVILY INVEST IN; ONE OF THE SIDE EFFECTS OF WHICH WILL BE … *WEIGHTLESSNESS*."

"*ALL* GOOD AND GREAT HUMAN FEATS AND WORKS ARE EMPOWERED AND FOLLOW AFTER THE EXERCISED, IF NOT MANIFESTLY RECOGNIZED … POWER OF DIVINE GRACE."

"I BELIEVE THAT EVERY YEAR OF HIS EIGHT YEAR ADMINISTRATION, GEORGE W. BUSH TESTED POSITIVE FOR IGNORANCE, WEAKNESS, ARROGANCE AND INCOMPETENCE—AND I CAN'T POSSIBLY ENVISION A SCENARIO, NOR CAN YOU, IN WHICH PUPPET MASTER AND VICE PRESIDENT DICK CHENEY, EVER CAME TO THE PUPPET PRESIDENT AND GROWLED … 'MR. PRESIDENT; I THINK WE OUGHT TO DO' THUS AND SUCH—AND GEORGE BUSH QUICKLY STOOD-UP WHILE SLAMMING HIS HAND ON HIS OVAL OFFICE DESK SAYING PASSIONATELY AND WITH CONVICTION; "NO DICK!"… WE'RE DEFINITELY, ABSOLUTELY AND UNEQUIVOCALLY—"NOT GOING TO DO THAT!"

... 'NOW GET YOUR ASS OVER HERE, SIT DOWN, SHUT-UP AND LET ME TELL YOU WHY!' ... DONALD TRUMP ON THE OTHER HAND ...?"

"THE MASTER TAUGHT US IN THE PARABLE OF *THE GOOD SAMARITAN*, THAT IT IS THOSE OF HUMANITY THAT ARE IN NEED THAT ARE OUR NEIGHBORS—AND WE'RE TO LOVE OUR NEIGHBOR AS OURSELVES—AND SINCE EVERYONE IS IN DIRE NEED (WHETHER THEY KNOW IT, BELIEVE IT, OR NOT); THEN OF NECESSITY AND BY EXTENSION ... *ALL* OF STRUGGLING MANKIND IS OUR NEIGHBOR."

"AS REGARDS THE NOBEL PEACE PRIZE BESTOWED UPON OBAMA; I BELIEVE THE NOBEL COMMITTEE SHOULD HAVE ALSO GIVEN "THE PRIZE" (AS A JOINT PRIZE) TO GEORGE BUSH JR. AND HIS EIGHT YEAR ADMINISTRATION OF MACHINATIONS AND SKULLDUGGERY, FOR MAKING IT POSSIBLE FOR BARACK H. OBAMA TO BECOME PRESIDENT OF THESE UNITED STATES OF AMERICA IN THE FIRST PLACE AND RECEIVE IT ... HAVING DONE NOTHING PRIOR TO HIS ELECTION THAT CAN BE PROVEN, OR AS OF YET TO WARRANT, WHAT HAS TURNED OUT TO BE, THE DAILY DIMINISHING HONOR OF OUR NATION UNDER A FLEDGLING PRESIDENT—AND MANIFESTLY EASILY MANIPULATED, INEXPERIENCED FIGUREHEAD OF A ONCE GREAT NATION GROWING WEAKER BY THE DAY UNDER HIS "HEROIC LEADERSHIP" AND ON HIS "ILLUSTRIOUS WATCH."

"FOR THOSE OF YOU WHO WERE WONDERING; WIPING IS NOT OPTIONAL AND "THE COURTESY FLUSH" <u>ISN'T</u> THE FINAL ONE AND ONLY."

"AMERICA HAS ALWAYS BEEN AMBIVALENT TOWARD FOREIGNERS AND IMMIGRANTS—AND WE

ALL KNOW AT LEAST ONE CONFLICTED POSTER CHILD FOR THE CAUSE NAMED–*KHMER GOWAY*."

"IN LIGHT OF THE REDEFINING OF THE TRADITIONAL AMERICAN FAMILY; I THINK THIS TIME I'M GOING TO BEAT THE LIBERAL EDUCATIONAL ELITE "SCHOLARS" TO THE DRAW, BY WRITING A PROGRESSIVE BESTSELLING CHILDREN'S BOOK ENTITLED:
WHY SALLY HAS FIVE MOMMIES NAMED BITCH AND A DADDY CALLED PIMP©."

"NOT ACTING UPON WHAT YOU BELIEVE DOESN'T MAKE IT UNTRUE; IT JUST MAKES YOU UNFAITHFUL."

"THESE DAYS' GLOBAL DIPLOMACY AND CUTTING-EDGE PROBLEM SOLVING SEEM TO HAVE BEEN REDUCED TO THE EFFECTIVENESS AND GASTRONOMIC EQUIVALENT OF A MINT LEAF BEING STRATEGICALLY PLACED ON A STEAMING HOT SHIT SANDWICH ... AND THAT ISN'T EXACTLY SWEETENING THE DEAL FOR ANYBODY."

"I'M SURE YOU'VE NOTICED BY NOW, THAT NOTHING DROPPED EVER LANDS AT YOUR FEET BUT ALWAYS ROLLS AWAY FROM YOU; FALLING OFF A SHEER CLIFF INTO THE ABYSS OR INTO DEEP FAST MOVING WATER, ROLLING FAR UNDERNEATH SOMETHING IMMOVABLE, OR THROUGH A SEWER GRATE TO OBLIVION—OR BOUNCING OFF INTO A BLACK HOLE IN A CORNER OF THE UNIVERSE NEVER TO BE SEEN AGAIN."

"NEVER VEGETATE OR DISSIPATE; ALWAYS AGGREGATE."

"HERE IN THE U.S.A. WE'VE ALWAYS PUT A WHOLE LOT OF COTTON RAG IN OUR (FOLDING) PAPER MONEY, BECAUSE 'COTTON IS KING'—AND IN AMERICA, '*COTTON IS THE FABRIC OF OUR LIVES.*'"

"THERE'S ONLY TWO HONORABLE WAYS YOU CAN STOP A MAN IN AMERICA FROM BECOMING PRESIDENT ... RUN AGAINST HIM AND WIN OR ELECT A WOMAN."

"STOP LOOKING BACK; YOUR FUTURE'S NOT BEHIND YOU."

"YOUNG PEOPLE, THE UNIVERSE IS CALLING YOU OUT; BRING YOUR GIFT WITH YOU."

"WE MAY NOT ALWAYS BE PRIVY TO THE ANSWERS, BUT WE KNOW THAT GOD IS ALWAYS ACTING UPON THE QUESTIONS."

"IT SEEMS IN MY LIFE AND SADLY SO; I HAVE TOO MANY KEYS TO DOORS THAT NO LONGER EXIST."

"ALCOHOL HAS THE STRONG TENDENCY TO SIMULTANEOUSLY LOOSEN ONE'S TONGUE AND HOBBLE THEIR INTELLECT."

"IF MISERY ACTUALLY LOVES COMPANY THEN THEY DESERVE EACH OTHER—BUT I BELIEVE THAT WHAT MISERY TRULY CRIES OUT FOR AND CONSTANTLY CRAVES, IS LOVE UNFEIGNED AND HOPE NO LONGER DEFERRED."

"THOUGH INDEED, LIFE WILL GO ON WITH OR
WITHOUT US; OFTEN TIMES THE QUESTION
BECOMES ... ARE WE WILLING TO FIGHT THE GOOD
FIGHT AND GO ON WITH LIFE?"

"THE REASON AMERICAN NATION BUILDING WILL
NEVER WORK IN MOSLEM COUNTRIES SUCH AS
IRAN, IRAQ, SYRIA AND AFGHANISTAN, IS
BECAUSE MOHAMMAD HAS BEATEN US TO THE
PUNCH AND HAS ALREADY BUILT FOR THEM A
NATION; NAMELY, THE UNEQUIVOCALLY
IRREVOCABLE *GLOBAL NATION OF ISLAM*."

"I LET THEM STAY, BECAUSE THE HUNGRY SPIDERS
HANGING FROM MY EAVES AND OUTSIDE MY
WINDOWS MAKE SURE THE CREEPY CRAWLERS
AND FLYING NASTIES NEVER MAKE IT TO THE
LIGHT, LET ALONE INTO MY HOUSE; JUST AS
PROVIDENCE MAKES CERTAIN THE RUPTURED
DEPARTING SOULS OF THE WICKED NEVER MAKE IT
TO GOD'S GREEN PASTURES OF PLENTY AND THE
UNAPPROACHABLE LIGHT OF GLORY ...
IN HIS HOUSE."

"I'M NOT VERY BIG ON EXHAUSTING MY
RESOURCES ON INTENSE PHYSICAL EXERTION
AND EXERCISE; I'M SAVING ALL MY ENERGY UP
FOR LONG LIFE."

"HE SAID; 'YOU SHALL *KNOW* THE TRUTH,
AND THE TRUTH SHALL MAKE YOU FREE.'
NOT MERELY KNOWING AND IGNORING IT,
OR KNOWING THE TRUTH AND DENYING IT,
NOR KNOWING IT AND SEEKING TO SUPPRESS
AND SUBVERT IT—BUT *KNOWING* IT, EMBRACING IT,
LOVING IT AND DEFENDING IT
SHALL MAKE YOU FREE."

"IN THIS PRESENT AGE SATAN WILL NEVER GO OFF
SOMEPLACE AND DIE, RATHER THAN USE HIS
ALLOTTED TIME TO TORMENT US YET-AGAIN."

"MY FRIEND, I'M HERE AND WILLING TO SERVE,
SO IF THERE'S ANYTHING I CAN DO FOR YOU
WITHIN MORAL AND LEGAL REASON,
DON'T HESITATE TO ASK."

"THOUGH IT WOULD BE A DEVASTATING BLOW TO
THE MICROWAVE INDUSTRY ... (AND LIKE I CARE)
I'M STILL MOVING FORWARD WITH MY IDEA TO
CREATE A PREMIUM, HIGH-END DESIGNER COFFEE
THAT ONCE HEATED, WILL MAINTAIN ITS INTERNAL
TEMPERATURE INDEFINITELY AND NEVER GET
COLD ... AND THE FINEST OF JAPANESE TEAS WILL
BE SOON TO FOLLOW."

"I'VE COME TO RECOGNIZE A SIGNIFICANT
PARALLEL BETWEEN THE EYE DISEASE GLAUCOMA
AND LEFT-WING ULTRA-LIBERALISM IN THE ARENA
OF HARDBALL POLITICS AND DECISION MAKING IN
AMERICA. FOR JUST AS GLAUCOMA IS CALLED THE
SNEAK-THIEF THAT ROBS US OF OUR SIGHT WITH
NO TIMELY PERCEPTION OF NOTICE, SUCKING IT
AWAY BY LITTLE AND LITTLE, SO TOO WILL
LIBERALISM UNCHECKED AND UNCHALLENGED
WHITTLE DOWN OUR COLLECTIVE PERIPHERAL
VISION AND RESOLVE AS WELL AS PRODUCING
MYOPIA—AND AS IT DOES, IT WILL DRAFT AWAY
THE WEALTH OF OUR HARD-WON LIBERTY AND
SUBSTANCE, WHILE CONSTRICTING OUR ABILITY
TO SEIZE EVEN THE DAY—LET ALONE SEE THE
FUTURE."

"ELDERLY PARENTS DON'T WANT FROM THEIR
ADULT CHILDREN THEIR GIFTS, THEY WANT THE
GIVERS—AND TRAGICALLY, SADLY AND

CONVERSELY, TOO MANY CHILDREN OF ELDERLY PARENTS WANT THEIR GIFTS ONLY, AND CARE NOTHING AND NO LONGER FOR THE AGED GIVER."

"THERE'S ONLY SO FAR A SQUINTING B-LIST ACTOR CAN GO IN HOLLYWOOD BITING A SMALL ITALIAN CIGAR, UTTERING A HANDFUL OF WORDS WHILE RIDING WITH A GRIMACE AND A SCOWL—AND CLINT EASTWOOD, GOD LOVE HIM, HAS APPARENTLY PROVEN UNEQUIVOCALLY THAT IT'S ALL THE WAY TO THE TOP ... AND DON'T EVEN GET ME STARTED ON RONALD REAGAN."

"NONE OF US HAVE MUCH CONTROL OVER THE WORLD IN WHICH WE LIVE, BUT WITHIN OUR PURVIEW, WE ALL HAVE SIGNIFICANT INFLUENCE IN THE LIVES OF THOSE WITH WHOM WE SHARE IT."

"AT MY AGE THERE'S ONLY SO FAST AND SO LONG I CAN BE EXPECTED TO KEEP RUNNING BACKWARDS WHILE DOING BACK FLIPS UP MULTIPLE STEEP FLIGHTS OF STAIRS CARRYING A HEAVY LOAD OF HOG-SHIT TO NOWHERE."

"SOMETIMES THINGS ARE EITHER OVER MY HEAD OR BENEATH MY DIGNITY TO CONSIDER."

"IN THIS LIFE TO OBTAIN CONTROL YOU ALWAYS HAVE TWO OPTIONS; YOU CAN EITHER LOWER THE 'FLAME' OR LIFT WHAT YOU'RE COOKING ABOVE AND AWAY FROM THE 'FIRE.'"

"I'VE NOTICED OF LATE, THAT THE SMOOTH AND HOMOGENOUS MELTING POT OF AMERICA TURNS AND SEPARATES INTO A THICK AND

CHUNKY STEW WHENEVER YOU TURN UP THE
HEAT LONG ENOUGH."

"THOUGH *ZEITGEIST* BY NATURE IS WHAT IT IS,
IT'S NOT NECESSARILY RIGHT."

"REGRETTABLY AND TRAGICALLY, WE ALL INHABIT
THIS PLANET EARTH WITH THE SELF-MADE BRUTAL
SAVAGES AND WELL-SCRUBBED MONSTERS THAT
SKULK AND DESIGN AS THEY NAVIGATE THE DARK
SIDE; WHO ARE ABLE TO LAUGH HEARTILY WITH US
BUT NEVER SMILE, BECAUSE THEIR CULTIVATED
ATTITUDE TOWARD HUMANITY HAS MADE THEM
MORE AND MORE LESS THAN HUMAN—AND THUS,
INFINITELY LESS MERCIFUL AND HUMANE—AND AN
EMINENT AND EVER-PRESENT THREAT AND
DANGER TO US ALL."

"I'M NOT A CHRISTIAN WRITER; I'M A WRITER
WHO HAPPENS TO BE A CHRISTIAN. THERE IS A
DISTINCT AND AT TIMES PROFOUND DIFFERENCE
YOU KNOW."

"WHAT HAVE I ACCOMPLISHED TODAY?
NOT MUCH ... BUT THAT'S MORE THAN USUAL."

"THEY WON'T HAVE TO DRAG ME OUT ...
IF I'M ABLE, I'LL WALK OUT ... AND IF IT'S THEIR
BULLETS OR THE FLAME OF THEIR FIRE THAT
SENDS ME TO GLORY ... I'LL THANK THEM FOR
THE RIDE."

"SOMETIMES OUR LIVES ARE A MOMENTARY
FIREFIGHT OF VIOLENT AND BLOODY CONFLICTED
FURY; OTHER TIMES, A PROTRACTED LIFELONG
GRINDING SIEGE OF LANGUISHING ATTRITION."

"I've noticed that when it comes to love and
romance everyone's looking to find and
harvest perfection, but rare few are
willing to cultivate it."

"If it breaks the heart of one who was
created in the image of God;
how could it not move and break the very
heart of God Himself?"

"The cry of the human heart has always
been … 'Acknowledge me!'"

"The rich and famous are either dead and in
heaven, or they're dead and in hell."

"In truth, one's death is not about anyone …
but oneself."

"'I want to see true; I don't want to see
anything that's not there."

"Sometimes you can't be creative to save
your freakin' life—
and no, it wasn't Picasso who said that …
it was me."

"You know what they say about men who are
short don't you? … 'They have to reach
higher to pull down the giants.'"

"Welcoming anyone into the clan on the
tender notion of emotion alone without
discernment, can be a very sketchy

PROPOSITION, BECAUSE WHEN YOU WELCOME THEM IN THUS, YOU NEVER KNOW BEFOREHAND WHAT YOU'RE GETTING ... THE APOSTLE PAUL, OR HANNIBAL LECTER."

"I KNOW WE'RE NOT EVOLVING BUT DEVOLVING AS THE HUMAN RACE, BECAUSE OF NECESSITY, WE'RE BECOMING MORE CREATIVE IN DEFENDING OURSELVES AGAINST OUR ENEMIES, BECAUSE OUR ENEMIES ARE BECOMING GREATER AND MORE CLEVER, WHICH MEANS WE ARE BECOMING WEAKER—AND WE ... ARE US."

"CHALLENGING THE MINDS OF THOSE THAT ARE CONFUSED IS MUCH MORE FUN THAN SIMPLY ANSWERING THEIR QUESTIONS."

"I'M NO CONNOISSEUR BY ANY STRETCH, BUT I DO LOVE FOODS THAT'RE HIGH IN FLAVOR AND NUTRITIONAL VALUE—AND LOW IN GAG REFLEX."

"WHEN YOU ATTEMPT TO INSULATE PEOPLE FROM THE INEVITABLE CHALLENGES, OFFENCES AND PAIN IN THEIR LIVES, YOU DENY THEM THE OPPORTUNITY TO BECOME GREAT AND THE CHANCE TO GROW STRONG ... 'SO TOUGH IT OUT, CUPCAKES!'"

"ALWAYS REMEMBER TO KEEP YOUR HOUSE CLEAN AND IN ORDER AND YOUR STERLING SILVERWARE AND FINE CHINA HANDY, BECAUSE YOU NEVER KNOW WHO'LL BE SHOWING UP FOR SUPPER FIRST—JESUS ... OR THE POPE."

"IF I COULD ABSOLUTELY AND PERFECTLY ORDER MY WORLD I PROBABLY WOULD—

AND I'D ALSO NO DOUBT BE SENDING IT BACK
WITHIN THE WEEK."

"SHE LOOKED ALL BUSTED-UP; WHAT THE HECK
DID SHE WANT DUDE?"
"WHINE."
"WHAT KIND OF WINE ... MERLOT, CABERNET,
RIESLING?"
"NO, THE BOO-HOO KIND."

"I'M NOT EXACTLY AN OPEN BOOK,
SO THOSE THAT WANT TO GET TO KNOW ME
MUST ABSOLUTELY LOVE TO READ."

"WHAT GOOD IS ANY MAN TO GOD, HIMSELF OR
OTHERS, IF HE ALLOWS HIMSELF TO BE
SHIPWRECKED AND CASTAWAY—STRANDED ON
THE ISLE OF OBLIVION?"

"THUS FAR MY LIFE SEEMS TO HAVE BEEN
NOTHING MORE THAN A PURELY PREPARATIVE
EXERCISE OF MUNDANE HOMEWORK IN MERE
HUMANITY—BUT ON THE UPSIDE AND IN LIGHT OF
THE FINAL EXAM AND ETERNITY ...
SO HAS EVERYONE ELSE'S."

"WE'LL ALL KNOW WHEN WE GET THERE TO BE
SURE, BUT HOW MANY OF US WILL COME TO FIND
THAT WE WERE WRONG?"

"FOR BETTER OR FOR WORSE, THE SPARK OF
DIVINITY WITHIN HUMANITY IS IMMORTALITY."

"A PERSON CAN ONLY BE JEALOUS IN ONE OF TWO
ARENAS; OVER WHAT LEGITIMATELY BELONGS TO

THEM, OR FOR WHAT LEGITIMATELY BELONGS TO SOMEBODY ELSE."

"BE ON GUARD; THOSE TRAPPED BY THE ENEMY MIGHT STILL BE THE ENEMY."

"LIGHT MAY DISPEL DARKNESS, BUT IT'S NOT GONNA STOP BULLETS."

"I WONDER ... WHICH IS MORE COMPELLING AND POWERFUL; USING WORDS TO PAINT A PICTURE, OR TELLING A STORY USING PAINT BRUSHED ON CANVAS."

"PEOPLE FEAR THE INSANE BECAUSE YOU CAN'T BLUFF THOSE THAT ARE CRAZY."

"GLOBALIZATION WAS AFOOT WHEN GOD CONFOUNDED THE LANGUAGES AND SCATTERED ALL HUMANITY AT THE TOWER OF BABEL— AND WE'RE TAP DANCING ON THE PRECIPICE ONCE AGAIN."

"MY NEIGHBORS ... YOU DON'T HAVE TO WORRY ABOUT THEM RAISING A RUCKUS AT ALL, BECAUSE BY THE TIME YOU WAKE UP AND GO TO WORK, THEY'LL STILL BE UNCONSCIOUS AND DEAD TO THE WORLD TILL WAY PAST NOON IN WHATEVER CONVENIENT CRIB THEY'VE CRASHED IN."

"'THE LORDS OF THE DRUG' ARE GETTING FABULOUSLY RICH RIDING THE TSUNAMI OF HUMANITY'S INSATIABLE LUST FOR EVER INCREASING DEGREES OF ALTERED STATES OF CONSCIOUSNESS."

"I DON'T HAVE TO CONCERN MYSELF WITH 'THE EYE IN THE SKY' AND THOSE WHO ARE WATCHING ME ... BECAUSE GOD IS WATCHING THEM."

"THAT 'THE BORROWER IS THE LENDERS SLAVE' IS AN ABSOLUTE TRUTH—AND ONE CAN'T BORROW FROM HIS MASTER TO PURCHASE HIS LOST LIBERTY, YET 'AMERICA THE PRODIGAL,' IS ATTEMPTING TO DO JUST THAT—AND IN SO DOING, IS CONDEMNING AND INDENTURING FUTURE GENERATIONS OF AMERICANS TO EVERMORE CONSTRICTING DEGREES OF HUMILIATING GLOBAL SERVITUDE AND BITTER BONDAGE."

"BY VIRTUE OF ITS VERY NATURE DEMOCRACY, AS WE NOW KNOW IT, WILL EVENTUALLY AND ALWAYS THREATEN MONOTHEISTIC RELIGIONS, BE THEY CHRISTIANITY, JUDAISM, ISLAM OR ANY OTHER— FOR DEMOCRACY IS BY DEFINITION MAJORITY RULE ... I.E. (IN PRACTICE) MOB RULE—AND GOD DOES NOT SPEAK AND GOVERN THROUGH THE MOB, NOR YIELD TO THE DECREE OF MAJORITY CONSENSUS."

"I HAVE A SIXTH SENSE AND IT'S OPERATIONAL, BUT IT ONLY KICKS IN WHEN MY OTHER FIVE SENSES ARE ALL DISABLED."

"THE <u>SOULS</u> OF ONLY <u>GOOD</u> <u>MEN</u> ARE <u>TRIED</u> BY THE <u>TIMES</u> IN WHICH THEY LIVE; THE BASE AND CRAVEN SUFFER NO SUCH CRISIS OF CONSCIENCE."

"IF THE LORD GOD OUR HEAVENLY FATHER ANSWERS YOUR PRAYERS THROUGHOUT YOUR LIFE IN EXCEEDINGLY ABUNDANT WAYS BECAUSE HE LOVES YOU AND YOU'VE ASKED HIM, REMEMBER; THE DAY MAY COME WHEN HE ASKS YOU TO DO SOMETHING FOR HIM—AND IT WOULD BE ILL

ADVISED AND EXTREMELY UNWISE IN THAT
MOMENT TO SAY 'NO,' TO YOUR ULTIMATE AND
ABSOLUTE ... 'GOD FATHER.'"

"IF YOU CHANGE SOMETHING AND THEN CHANGE IT
BACK AGAIN, ARE THERE ANY CHANGES?"

"DON'T MESS WITH PERFECTION ... AND IF YOU DO
MESS WITH IT, WHEN YOU FIND YOURSELF TO BE IN
THE WRONG; GO BACK, BEG ITS FORGIVENESS AND
DON'T MAKE THE SAME MISTAKE AGAIN."

"CONSIDERING SOME OF THE STUFF I SAY, DO AND
WRITE ... I'VE GOT TO BE KIDDING MYSELF!"

"I'M JUST SAYIN', YOU'LL REALLY WANNA STAY
AWAY FROM VACATIONING IN ANY OF THOSE THIRD
WORLD HOT-SPOTS WHERE WHEN THE 'POLICE'
WANT TO TAKE YOU IN AND HAVE A 'LITTLE TALK'
IN PRIVATE, IT NECESSITATES SURGICAL
INSTRUMENTS RUBBER GLOVES, SODIUM
PENTOTHAL AND A SWINGING LIGHT BULB."

"I'D REFRAIN FROM USING AND BRAGGING ON THE
TERM *MANIFEST DESTINY* TO DESCRIBE AND
JUSTIFY AMERICA'S MEANS OR HER MOTIVES,
FOR THE CONSEQUENCES OF BOTH HAVE NOT YET
BEEN FULLY REALIZED."

"DON'T BE SURPRISED; HELL IS FULL OF PEOPLE
WHO DON'T BELIEVE IN HELL."

"I'M ALMOST ALWAYS GOOD NATURED AND EASY GOING, BUT IF PUSHED HARD ENOUGH AND NEED BE—I CAN BE AS SERIOUS, DANGEROUS AND LIFE THREATENING AS AN UNKNOWN STRAIN OF FLESH-EATING BACTERIA ... AND SO COULD YOU."

"THESE DAYS EVERYONE WANTS TO MAKE A STATEMENT, AND THE ONLY TRULY PROFOUND STATEMENT MOST HAVE TO MAKE IS ... 'I'VE GOT NOTHING ORIGINAL TO SAY.'"

"WE SECURE AND MAINTAIN EQUILIBRIUM IN OUR LIVES BY MINIMIZING THE EFFECTS OF THOSE THINGS WE DON'T HAVE CONTROL OVER, BY MAXIMIZING CONTROL OVER THE THINGS WE DO."

"IT'S THE CONDITION OF OUR HEART AND MOTIVES <u>AT THE TIME WE ACT</u> THAT GOD'S CONCERNED ABOUT AND WILL JUDGE; NOT HOW 'PERFECTLY' <u>IN OUR OPINION</u> OUR EFFORT SEEMS TO HAVE TURNED OUT IN THE END."

"HUMAN BEINGS ARE SHEEP WITHOUT A SHEPHERD AND THE WOLVES AMONG US KNOW IT."

"I BELIEVE, ACCORDING TO MY SOURCES, THAT THE REAL REASON SIMON AND GARFUNKEL BROKE UP WAS BECAUSE OF THEIR ARTISTIC DISPUTE OVER THE LYRICS OF THEIR OH SO MELLOW SONG *SCARBOROUGH FAIR*—FOR APPARENTLY, ART GARFUNKEL, A GOURMET COOK IN HIS OWN RIGHT WITH A PENCHANT FOR ITALIAN CUISINE, WAS QUITE ADAMANT ABOUT WANTING THE LYRICAL REFRAIN TO BE ... "PARSLEY, SAGE, ROSEMARY AND *OREGANO* PRECEDING THE LINE— *"SHE ONCE WAS, A FRIEND OF A GIGOLO"*—AND PAUL SIMON ... NOT SO MUCH ... WHO'D A THUNK IT?"

"GOD WILLING I'LL DO WHAT I CAN, UP TO AND
INCLUDING MY VERY LIFE."

"WHEN I WAS A KID I WISH I WOULD'VE HAD
SOMEONE LIKE ME IN MY LIFE."

"BETTER TO BE ALONE AND LONELY,
THAN WITH SOMEONE AND LONELY."

"DON'T GET TOO COMFORTABLE WE'RE NOT
MEANT TO BE HERE FOREVER."

"IT'S AMAZING HOW MUCH LIBERTY WE HAVE TO
CHOOSE THE LIVES WE WANT
AND THEN LOATHE THE LIVES WE GET."

"I'VE COME TO REALIZE THAT WRITER'S BLOCK IS
ESSENTIALLY CONSTIPATION OF THE
IMAGINATION."

"I AGREE THAT TOFU IS GOOD FOR YOU AND
HEALTHFUL; ESPECIALLY WHEN IT ACCOMPANIES
A TWO INCH THICK, 24OZ. MELT IN YOUR MOUTH
GRILLED-FIRE-SEARED KOBE PORTERHOUSE
STEAK, A POUND AND A HALF-BAKED IDAHO
POTATO TOPPED WITH SWEET CREAM BUTTER AND
CHIVES, SOUR CREAM AND UNLIMITED SLICES OF
THICK, PAN-FRIED DOUBLE SMOKED BACON, A
GIANT *BLOOMING VIDALIA ONION*—AND ALL OF IT
WASHED DOWN WITH A BIG FAT FROSTY MUG OF
PREMIUM ICE COLD JUST *SHY OF SLUSH* AMERICAN
BEER ... 'TO YOUR HEALTH!' ... 'ENJOY!'"

"I DON'T NEED MY HEAD SHRUNK;
JUST TWEAKED A BIT."

"Unlike some pristine upscale neighborhoods, I like my mom's postage stamp parcel of backyard, because it's not ostentatiously manicured, contrived or ornamental; it's just denuded, low maintenance hard-packed erosion."

"The only dream I remember was waking-up— and when I woke up ... I was still sleeping."

"Just like the word *infuse*, I love the word *extrude*—and I've always wanted to use them in a quote—and now ... I have."

"'Hope springs eternal,' but it's not always mutual."

"Punching an extra hole in the business end of your belt I've found is an anti-incentive for losing weight."

"I wouldn't say I don't have an interest in women; I have no woman in my life I have an interest in."

"Perhaps the world's always been dysfunctional, but I'm just now noticing it because I'm now responsible for a significant slice of it; the world that is, not the dysfunction."

"On my block when I was a kid and tempers flared, you'd risk a black eye, fat lip or bruised ribs which were the order of the

DAY; NOW WHEN SOMEONE GETS DISSED, GLOCKS AND MAC 10S GET WHIPPED-OUT IN THE HOOD."

"IT'S ALL HEMORRHAGING—AND THE PHILOSOPHY AND STRATEGY OF THE WORLD AT LARGE SEEMS TO HAVE BEEN REDUCED TO: 'IF IT'S LEAKING, LET'S NOT FIX IT; LET'S JUST PUT A BUCKET UNDER IT AND SAY WE DID.'"

"IF I CAN'T HAVE WHAT I WANT, I'D RATHER NOT HAVE WHAT I DON'T."

"VILLAINS' ARE RARELY MANIFESTED UNTIL THEY ACT AND SUCCEED."

"REGRETTABLY AND SAD TO SAY, MOST OF US LOVERS HAVE TO SETTLE FOR A MATCH MADE JUST A LITTLE LOWER HEAVEN."

"WE IN THE WESTERN WORLD GENERALLY AND AMERICA IN PARTICULAR, HAVE REDUCED OURSELVES TO THE PURSUIT OF MERE FOOD AND ENTERTAINMENT, BREAD AND CIRCUS; EPICUREAN SPECTATORS IN A WORLD WITH HORDES OF HUNGRY BARBARIANS AT OUR GATES, CROSSING THROUGH THE BREECH IN OUR WALL WITH NO CLARION TRUMPET SOUNDING."

"THERE'S NO FOURTH OPTION; YOU'RE EITHER DEAD, OR ALIVE, OR SCHRÖDINGER'S CAT."

"YOU MAY WELL GET YOUR WAY—AND STILL NOT GET WHAT YOU WANT."

"OFTEN GUYS AT MY AGE ARE SIMPLY THINKING ABOUT RIDING OFF INTO THE SUNSET; OTHERS ... FADING TO BLACK."

"AS HUMAN BEINGS, NONE OF US CAN LONG LIVE PAIN AND CAREFREE LOTUS EATING LIVES OF PEACE AND COMFORT—ALL OF US HAVING BEEN HARDWIRED FOR THORNS AND THISTLES, THE CONSTANT CRAVING FOR ADRENALIN—AND WAITING FOR THE OTHER SHOE TO DROP."

"SUICIDE IS NOT AN ESCAPE; IT IS A COMPROMISE OF DESPAIR, COWARDICE AND HOPE."

"SOMETIMES THE NEXT MOVE WE'RE WAITING FOR IS OUR OWN."

"FATHERS REALLY NEED TO ASK THEMSELVES ... 'WOULD I WANT MY DAUGHTER TO MARRY A MAN LIKE ME?'"

"IF YOU'RE WAITING FOR THE PLAYING FIELD TO BE LEVEL BEFORE YOU GET INTO THE GAME ... YOU'VE ALREADY LOST."

"THE REWARD FOR JUST KEEPING YOUR HEAD ABOVE THE WAVES IS LIFE AND NOT DROWNING— AND YOU CAN DECIDE IF IT'S WORTH THE EFFORT."

"THESE DAYS WE ALL HAVE ACCESS TO INCREDIBLE HUMAN KNOWLEDGE, THOUGH NOT ENOUGH DIGESTIVE MENTAL JUICES TO DISSOLVE ALL THE CHUNKS AND FRAGMENTS INTO WISDOM."

"Girls, you don't want to marry a man who
thinks everything he eats
is just a delivery system for garlic."

"Like the Prodigal Son, I want to make
it through this life no worse for wear
but wiser."

"I suspect throughout history more Bibles
have succumbed to over-thumping,
injudicious use of Lemon Pledge and dust
mites, than needed to be replaced due to
illegible finger soiled and tearstained
pages."

"My job has morphed into a recipe for
disaster, and I'm the main ingredient."

"I perceive humanity is heading into a meat
grinder with no off switch."

"I don't mind being the punctuation in the
lives of others, but I don't want to be the
addendum in anyone's life."

"Yah, you only live once ... but it's forever."

"I've come to realize that most people smile
when they're happy, high, or deranged."

"We're either living in the reality that's
being created for us by others,
or we're actively involved in creating it
ourselves."

"WHEN THE CONFLAGRATION OF RUINOUS RIOT IN
THE STREETS OF THE BIG AND FAT-CITY IS FINALLY
OVER, AND THE INCITERS, SUBVERSIVES AND
PERPETRATORS ARE BEING DILIGENTLY SOUGHT
OUT FOR HEAD-THUMPIN'; I'LL BET YOU
PAYCHECKS AND CAN GUARANTEE YOU THAT—*YOU
WON'T* FIND THE AUSTRALIAN, SWEDISH,
CANADIAN OR JAPANESE KID IN A ROYAL ASS-
TANGLE AT THE BOTTOM OF THE GOOSE PILE."

"IF A MAN LIVES A BASE LIFE THAT COUNTS FOR
NOTHING IN THE EYES OF GOD, AT LEAST HIS
DEATH SHOULD—AND IF HE DESIRES AND WILLS TO
BE WOOED AT HIS LAST BREATH <u>LIKE THE THIEF ON
THE CROSS</u> NEXT TO OUR LORD JESUS, THEN HIS
LIFE AT LAST AND AFTER ALL WILL BE DEEMED BY
THE DIVINE ... A STUNNING SUCCESS!"

"I'M QUITE SURE THE LYRICS ARE ... "ME AND YOU
AND A DOG NAMED BOO"—NOT ...
ME AND YOU AND A JEW NAMED SHMU."

"WHEN THE POPE FINALLY DECLARED THAT ALL
CATHOLICS COULD EAT MEAT ON FRIDAYS,
I RAN IT BY MY FATHER WHO SAID ... 'WE'RE NOT
UNDER THE *POPE OF ROME*, WE'RE GREEK
ORTHODOX AND UNDER THE PATRIARCH IN
CONSTANTINOPLE—
'<u>SO YOU TAKE YOUR ORDERS FROM ME!</u>'"

"I ALWAYS THOUGHT THAT FREDERICK DOUGLAS
LOOKED MEAN, BECAUSE I NEVER SAW A PHOTO
OF HIM SMILING—BUT THEN AGAIN, COME TO THINK
OF IT, I NEVER SAW A PICTURE OF GEORGE
WASHINGTON OR ABRAHAM LINCOLN GRINNING
LIKE HOUND DOGS EATING SHIT-OUT-OF-A-BROOM
EITHER."

"I'M NOT BADMOUTHING THIS COUNTRY PER SE;
I'M BADMOUTHING THIS WHOLE TWISTED WORLD
SYSTEM, FOR AS GOES THE UNITED STATES,
SO GOES THE WORLD IN TOW—AND IT'S A
DISGRACEFUL PITEOUS SHAME, THAT WE'RE
NOW ABLE TO HONESTLY SAY ...
'WE WERE *ONCE* AMERICA.'"

"IF GOD OUR HEAVENLY FATHER SAW FIT THAT
HIS SON, OUR LORD AND SAVIOR JESUS CHRIST'S
FIRST MIRACLE ON THIS EARTH AT A WEDDING IN
CANA OF GALILEE, WAS TO TURN MERE WATER
INTO <u>160 GALLONS</u> OF THE MOST EXCELLENT
WINE—SIMPLY BECAUSE THE FOLKS RAN OUT AND
HIS DISCIPLES WANTED IT ... WHO AM I TO BE A
TEETOTALER?"

"NOMINAL MOSLEMS LIKE NOMINAL CHRISTIANS
ARE NO THREAT TO ANYONE'S KINGDOM."

"DON'T GET FRUSTRATED WHEN YOU GET COCK-
BLOCKED ON YOUR WAY TO DOING SOMETHING
WRONG ... COUNT IT A BLESSING."

"DON'T LAUGH KID, I'VE EARNED THIS FACE;
YOU'VE YET TO EARN YOURS."

"I LIKE TO KNOW WHERE MY COPY PAPER COMES
FROM, BECAUSE I'M CURIOUS AS TO WHICH
RAINFOREST—BRAZILIAN OR INDONESIAN IS
ENDING UP IN THE LOCAL LANDFILL."

"CHILD, DON'T ALLOW YOURSELF TO GROW UP TO
BE A THREATENING BEING, OR A BEING THAT
ALLOWS THEMSELVES TO BE THREATENED;

LAY A PREEMPTIVE HAND ON NO MAN, NOR SUFFER YOURSELF TO BE LAID A HAND ON."

"I HAVE LIMITS, AND I'M MORE THAN WILLING TO DRAW LINES, BUT SOMETIMES I HAVE TO WAIT TILL I GET THERE TO DO SO."

"IT'S REALLY QUITE DISCOURAGING AND DISCONCERTING WHEN THE CROWS IN YOUR LIFE ARE TWICE AS BIG AS THE EAGLES THEY'RE CHASING."

"VERY MUCH UNLIKE THE SECRET SERVICE THROWING A SMOKING MANNLICHER CARCANO RIFLE INTO THE HANDS OF LEE HARVEY OSWALD ON THAT TRAGIC DAY IN NOVEMBER AND SAYING ... 'YOU DID IT.'—I COULDN'T SEE MYSELF JUST GRABBING AT RANDOM ANY OF THE WOMEN THAT HAD BEEN BROUGHT INTO MY LIFE THUS FAR AND SAYING, 'YOU'RE IT.'... OR, 'YOU'RE THE ONE FOR ME'—BECAUSE IT'S NOT AS SIMPLE AS ALL THAT, MY BABIES."

"FOR BETTER OR FOR WORSE; DEATH UNIQUELY AND UNEQUIVOCALLY HAS THE POWER TO ANSWER THE QUESTIONS THAT MORTAL LIFE NEVER COULD."

"LET OUR SCARS NEVER DEFINE US BUT MERELY REMIND US."

"THE DEAD ARE ALWAYS SO PEACEFUL AND STILL, BUT NOT ALL OF THEM AT REST."

"FRANKLY, SEEING AS THEY GET TO HAVE AND
ENJOY SEVENTY-TWO VIRGINS FOR ALL ETERNITY, I
SEE NO PROBLEM WHATSOEVER WITH THE
MOSLEMS WANTING TO PUT ME, OR FOR THAT
MATTER ANY OTHER WESTERN GUY UNDER SOME
SMOKING HOT BABE NAMED SHARIA LAW—AS
LONG AS SHARIA'S ALSO A SINGLE YOUNG
CHRISTIAN GIRL WHO WANTS TO GET MARRIED
AND KNOWS HOW TO COOK."

"THIS IS THE EARTH WE INHABIT—AND THE ONLY
INTELLIGENT MONSTERS HERE ARE HUMAN—
AND THE NEFARIOUS AND PERNICIOUS SPIRITS
THAT INSPIRE THEM."

"I DON'T WANT TO LET ANYONE 'SEDUCE' ME AND
THEN CLAIM IN DEFENSIVE PROTEST THAT, 'I WAS
BEGUILED'—AND NEITHER SHOULD YOU, BECAUSE
IT'S NOT SEDUCTION, <u>IF YOU WANT</u> IT TO HAPPEN."

"<u>ALMOST</u> GETTING SOMEONE KILLED ISN'T THE
SAME AS SAVING THEIR LIFE."

"SORRY PAL, BUT I'M AN AMERICA; I SHOULDN'T
HAVE TO, NOR DO I, LOOK OVER MY SHOULDER
WHENEVER I'M WALKING DOWN THE STREET—
AND I'VE GOT NOTHING TO HIDE,
SO I MIGHT AS WELL WALK LIKE A MAN
THAT KNOWS HE'S FREE."

"NOT TO BELABOR THE ISSUE, BUT HAVE THESE
DEEP-FRIED MOSTLY ILLITERATE NUT-BALLS EVER
CONSIDERED THE FACT THAT, JUST MAYBE, DUE TO
MANY CENTURIES OF TRANSMISSION AND
MISTRANSLATION OF THE SACRED TEXT AND LOTS
OF TESTOSTERONE STEEPED WISHFUL THINKING—
AND IF THERE'S ALSO ANY MORAL SANITY AND

JUSTICE LEFT IN THIS WORLD, THAT IT MAY NOT BE
SEVENTY-TWO VIRGINS FOR ALL OF ETERNITY, BUT
MERELY ONE, SEVENTY TWO OLD VIRGIN OF
INDETERMINATE GENDER?"

[WHAT DR. SPIN NEEDS TO KNOW] ...
"MR. PRESIDENT, I CAN UNDERSTAND YOU
WANTING TO TIE-UP ALL THE LOOSE ENDS ON THIS
HEMORRHAGING FIASCO, BUT JUST HOW HIGH AND
FAR UP YOUR ASS DO YOU WANT ME TO GO TO WIPE
THIS THING?"

"IT'S NICE TO BE REMEMBERED,
BUT IT'S BETTER TO BE KNOWN."

"AS A WRITER, I DON'T ALWAYS EXPECT PEOPLE
TO AGREE WITH ME AND WHAT I WRITE AND SAY,
BUT I WOULD HOPE THEY'D BE WILLING TO
SERIOUSLY ASK THEMSELVES ... 'WHY?'"

"*THE UGLY AMERICAN* WOULD'VE HAD NO
PROBLEM WHATEVER GOING UNABASHEDLY
TO TOKYO WITH A GAS-POWERED LEAF BLOWER
DURING THE *SAKURA MATSURI* (CHERRY BLOSSOM
VIEWING FESTIVAL) ... AND ALL THE WHILE
THINKING HE'S DOING THE JAPANESE A HUGE
FAVOR."

"SOME DAYS YOU SUCCEED AT ACCOMPLISHING
NOTHING BUT LOSS."

"IF YOU CATCH ON FIRE ... 'BY ALL MEANS DON'T
RUN!'—STOP, DROP AND ROLL ... UNLESS OF
COURSE, YOU FIND YOURSELF STANDING IN A POOL
OF GASOLINE OR A ROOM LOADED WITH
GUNPOWDER."

"Your life is a gift that needs to be given—
not simply received."

"'It's Good to Touch the Green Green
'Grass' of Home' ... especially if you live on
the island of Maui ... 'Wowie!'"

"In this our modern society and culture
food has become therapy and
entertainment, drink has become a crutch,
sex has become purely recreational, truth
has become relative and reality has become
optional."

"When it comes to us saving the Earth's
fragile and imploding environment
and global ecosystem we've been told,
'You have until TODAY to get it done' and
'today' ... was yesterday."

"Sometimes acting upon and living by faith,
makes one feel like a spider lowering itself
into a bottle and then cutting the last
gleaming wisp of its silken lifeline."

"God will always send the light to be where
He needs the light to be ... into the
darkness; the Zeitgeist spewing emotional
and spiritual vomit notwithstanding."

"You'll be amazed at what you can do with a
sharp knife and mortified by what you can't
do with a dull one."

"God the Son *the son of man*, made the sons
of men *the sons of God*."

"In the hood, tying a yellow ribbon round
the old oak tree ought not to be confused
with tying yellow police tape around the
old homestead."

"When eating out my philosophy is …
don't order anything that has too many
moving parts."

"There's a significant difference between
pleasure and satisfaction,
for the former rarely accomplishes
the latter."

"If you're a loser who seeks to silence the
opposition and you succeed …
you've become a successful loser."

"Adultery at its very core is stealing, for
it's taking something that doesn't belong to
you, as well as receiving something that the
giver has no right to give."

"War may not be the answer, but it is at
times the only reasonable reply."

"Deliverance isn't necessarily an event but
a process—and if you're willing to endure
the process … you'll eventually be free."

"Fasting is the earnest pursuit of that
which can't be remedied or attained
by mere food, drink and entertainment."

"Peace on the mountaintop is a given; you
have to work at having peace in the valley."

"I don't really care how appealing to the
eye or how neatly they're stacked …
I want them fresh!"

"A pearl never ceases to be an irritation to
the oyster, or it would cease to be a pearl."

"I'd rather devote my life to creating
beauty than mitigating ugliness."

"The spirit of man is troubled by many
things and comforted by few."

"Addictions are diverse and complex; having
one thing in common … the addicted."

"If I need cast myself down, I would have it
at God's mercy and man's judgement …
rather than the reverse."

"History knows and has seen everything
but rarely spills her guts at first blush;
the future has seen nothing,
yet promises us vision."

"IT'S A CATCH-22 FOR REAL; THE UP SIDE OF WEARING A HOODIE IS THAT WHEN YOU'RE UP TO SOMETHING NO GOOD, THEY CAN'T SEE YOU AND IDENTIFY YOUR FACE; THE DOWN SIDE IS, YOU CAN'T SEE-UM COMING UP BEHIND YOU WITH BASEBALL BATS AND CROWBARS—AND WHEN THEY'RE DONE WITH YOU AND THE POLICE SHOW-UP AND FINALLY PULL OFF YOUR HOODIE; THEY STILL WON'T BE ABLE TO RECOGNIZE OR IDENTIFY YOUR FACE."

"I'VE COME TO REALIZE THAT CHRISTIANITY IS IN VERY DEED EXCLUSIVE ... AND THAT BY DIVINE DESIGN—AND ALLOWS FOR NO WIGGLE ROOM WHATSOEVER—THUS REDUCING AND IN FACT ELIMINATING THE PLETHORA OF DIVERSE, CONFUSING AND CONFLICTING INTELLECTUAL ARGUMENTS, HUMAN OPINIONS AND OPTIONS, TO MERELY ONE SIMPLY BRILLIANT AND BOLD, ELEGANTLY STUNNING CHOICE—AND THUS, EXCLUDING ONLY AND ALL, THOSE WHO ARE NOT WILLING TO LEAVE THE DARKNESS AND COME TO ... THE LIGHT."

"IF YOU KEEP SPENDING YOUR TIME IN VENUES THAT ARE MINDLESS, YOU'LL STOP THINKING."

"IF YOU'RE DRUNK AND NAVIGATING ON FOOT, YOU'RE JUST LOOKING FOR THE NEXT EDGE TO HANG ON TO."

"MY CLAIM TO FAME HAS ALWAYS BEEN THAT I CAN PACK THIRTY POUNDS OF SHIT INTO A TEN-POUND BAG."

"IT'S HARD TO SAY BECAUSE THE VAGARIES OF MY JOB ARE SUCH, THAT IF I DIDN'T HEAR WHAT THEY SAID, IT COULD'VE BEEN BECAUSE I WAS LISTENING TO WHAT THEY DIDN'T SAY."

"LET MY TEARS BE THE BALM THAT HEALS MY EYES THAT THEY MIGHT SEE CLEARLY."

RULES OF FREEDOM CAPTURE AND ESCAPE

1.) DON'T DO ANYTHING FOR WHICH YOU'LL NEED TO BE CAPTURED.
2.) IF YOU DO ... DON'T GET CAUGHT.
3.) IF YOU ARE APPREHENDED; ESCAPE AS QUICKLY AND CLEANLY AS POSSIBLE.
4.) IF YOU CAN'T ESCAPE IMMEDIATELY, MAKE ALL YOUR CAPTORS WISH TO JESUS YOU HAD.

"BY ALL MEANS PUT YOUR MONEY WHERE YOUR HEART IS, BUT NEVER LAY YOUR HEART TO REST WHERE YOUR MONEY LIES."

"LET SUCCESS BE YOUR DRUG OF CHOICE AND CREATIVITY YOUR DEALER."

"EVERYONE WANTS A PIECE OF YOU—AND IT'S NOT ALWAYS A PIECE YOU CAN AFFORD TO GIVE-UP."

"I WAS GIVEN A REAL NICE HIGH QUALITY FITTED BASEBALL CAP WITH A LOGO FROM A BREWERY THAT BURNT-DOWN TO THE GROUND AND NO LONGER EXISTS; SO I'M GUESSING IT'S OKAY TO WEAR IT TO SUNDAY MORNING GO-TO-MEETIN'."

"TONGUE TWISTER: (THREE TIMES FAST) 'TWILL
COOL QUICKLY RIPLEY.'"

"I DON'T LIKE THE IDEA OF 'THROWING LEAD,'
BECAUSE IT'S RECIPROCAL."

"THE SWORD OF ISLAM HAS PROVEN ITSELF TO BE
A BLOODY AND BLUNT INSTRUMENT—
AS THE SHARP SWORD OF THE WEST HAS BEEN
SHEATHED."

"NO ONE ESCAPES PAIN; DOING BATTLE WILL TAKE
ITS TOLL, EVEN ON THE VICTORS."

"IF GOD IS *MERELY* MY CO-PILOT, THEN HE'S THE
ONLY ONE NO BOARD THAT'S *NOT* IN TROUBLE."

"WHAT CHICKENS LACK IN INTELLIGENCE,
THEY MORE THAN MAKE UP FOR IN DEEP-FRIED
TASTY GOODNESS."

"'DON'T WORRY ABOUT IT PAL!' ... YOU LOOK LIKE
YOU'VE SEEN DEATH ITSELF AND YOU'RE SHAKING
LIKE A CHIHUAHUA SHITTING PEACH-PITS, SO I
REPEAT ... A WOMAN WAS MADE TO PLEASE A MAN
AND A MAN HAS BEEN MADE TO GIVE A WOMEN
SOMEONE TO PLEASE—BUT THE JURY'S STILL OUT
AND THE MATH'S A BIT FUZZY ON THE DYNAMIC OF
THE CURRENT DISCONNECT, SINCE THAT UGLY
APPLE INCIDENT IN THE GARDEN ... 'DUDE! ...
SHE'S STANDING RIGHT BEHIND ME, ISN'T SHE?'"

"FOR THE VAST MAJORITY OF HUMANITY THERE'LL
BE NO PEACE, ONLY EPHEMERAL DIVERSIONS."

"THE ONLY THING THAT MAKES IT POSSIBLE FOR
ME TO BE A SUCCESSFUL WRITER IS THE FACT
THAT I'M COMPUTER GENERATED."

"BUDDY, I'M GOING TO DO YOU A SOLID AND GIVE
YOU THE HEADS-UP ... THEY DON'T CALL HER VAL
BECAUSE HER NAME'S VALERIE; THEY CALL HER
VAL BECAUSE IT'S SHORT FOR VALTREX®."

"SOMETIMES A GIFT IS HARDER TO LET GO OF THEN
SOMETHING YOU'VE WORKED HARD TO EARN."

"IT'S NOT THE SIZE OF THE 'DOG' IN THE FIGHT;
IT'S THE SIZE OF THE BULLET THAT EVENTUALLY
GETS PUNCHED THROUGH HIS RABID SKULL
TO FINALLY PUT HIM DOWN."

"WHEN THE UNCERTAINTY OF THE CERTAINTY
OF A MAN'S DAY COMES WHY WOULD HE CLUTCH
AT STRAWS, WHILE HE CAN STILL CLEAVE TO THE
CROSS OF GRACE AT CALVARY? FOR THE *TWO*
RAW EDGES OF A WOUND MUST CLING TO ONE
ANOTHER TO CLOSE THE BREACH AND BE
HEALED—THE WOUNDS OF OUR BROKEN
HUMANNESS AND THE WOUNDS OF OUR SAVIOR
MUST BE MADE ONE ON THESE *OUR* SHORES,
BEFORE WE CAN CONQUER *THE OTHER* ...
GREAT DIVIDE."

"GOT STIMULANTS?" ...
COUNCIL OF COLUMBIAN 'COFFEE' GROWERS."

"I WOULD LOVE TO SEE MY SUBORDINATES AT
WORK HAVE AN EPIPHANY—AND IF NOT ...
A TRANSFER *OUT*, WILL DO NICELY."

"You see ... *that's* how old men get hurt;
they think they still are what they *never*
once were ... and act on it."

"A recruiter for suicide/homicide bombers
answering questions and giving a young
perspective 'martyr' the spiel ... 'Well no,
it's not actually in the Koran, but dude—
do you *really* want to start pulling at
that thread?'"

"Any African American man or woman who
refers to other blacks as 'niggers,' uses
the word freely and then claims in
defensive protest that ... 'We now own the
word,' is like a freed slave who inherits a
whip from his former master—and then uses
it to beat his former fellow slaves—and no
catharses, nor any good thing will ever
come from the employment and driving-in of
yet another self-segregating ...
'ethnic wedge.'"

"*Bitching* like struggling is a sign of life,
because nothing struggles to die,
everything struggles to live."

"I don't believe God ever intended for man
to have any reason whatsoever to move
faster than he can on horseback ...
however, the idea of wormholes in the
universe and inter-dimensional
transporters do intrigue me."

"Man, I'm not a fighter I'm a writer ...
but then again—a writer's just a fighter
who's taken off his gloves so he can type."

"I DON'T BELIEVE THAT RUNNING OR ANY OTHER PHYSICAL EXERCISE WILL ADD YEARS TO YOUR LIFE, OR FOR THAT MATTER LIFE TO YOUR YEARS ... I JUST WANT MY PANTS TO FIT."

"SAY NO TO GOD? ... NONE OF US IS STRONG ENOUGH TO BE THAT FOOLISH."

"OUR DEVICES PROVE THAT THESE DAYS EVERYONE WANTS THEIR LIFE KEPT IN A NEAT LITTLE BUNDLE—AND THE DOWNSIDE OF THAT IS, IF YOU PUT ALL YOUR SHIT IN ONE BAG, IT MIGHT JUST SOMEDAY ALL GET KNOCKED OVERBOARD INTO THE CHOP."

"AN OLD MAN ONCE TOLD ME WHEN I WAS YOUNG—'YOU'VE GOT TO TRY BOY, KEEP ON MOVING AND DON'T QUIT.' AND YOU KNOW, HE WAS RIGHT, BECAUSE I'VE NOTICED IN RETROSPECT, THAT THE STINGING BUGS AND NASTIES I'VE BEEN ABLE TO KILL IN MY LIFE, WERE THOSE THAT DIDN'T JUMP OR FLY, DIDN'T JUMP OR FLY FAR ENOUGH AWAY, DIDN'T JUMP OR FLY FAST ENOUGH, OR DIDN'T KEEP ON JUMPING AND FLYING."

"THROUGHOUT THE WORLD AND HUMAN HISTORY, FOOD AND DRINK HAVE ALWAYS BEEN CONSIDERED A REASON FOR AND OCCASION OF THANKSGIVING, REJOICING AND CELEBRATION, BUT IN THE MODERN WESTERN WORLD AND THE UNITED STATES IN PARTICULAR, WE'VE MADE FOOD AN ENEMY TO OUR BODIES AND HEALTH THAT HAS TO BE DEFEATED—AND WHEN YOU MAKE FOOD AND DRINK YOUR ENEMY ...
IT WILL BE."

"I'M PRETTY SURE THAT SALVADOR DALI AND THE
DALI LAMA ARE ONLY RELATED BY RUMOR."

"I WANT TO SEE CLEARLY, I WANT TO SEE FAR, AND
I WANT TO SEE FOR A LONG, LONG TIME."

"TOO MANY OF OUR LIVES ARE HOT MESSES THAT
NEED TO BE EDITED, BEFORE THEY FALL INTO THE
HANDS OF ... 'THE PUBLISHER.'"

"ONCE THEY DEVELOP 'THE AMAZING APP,'
I'M SURE EVERYONE'LL BE TEXTING GRACE
BEFORE MEALS AT THE TABLE ... AND 'HOW SWEAT
THE SOUND.'"

"IF I WOULD MAKE A MARK IN THIS LIFE, I WOULD
HAVE IT DEEP, SHARP AND CLEAN."

"THE IDEA OF RETIRING DOESN'T MUCH APPEAL TO
ME; THE NOTION HOWEVER OF NOT DOING WHAT
I'VE BEEN DOING FOR THE PAST THIRTY YEARS TO
EARN A LIVING DOES."

"THE ENDS ONLY JUSTIFY THE MEANS IF BOTH
ARE JUST."

"THERE'S A MELANCHOLY IN REMEMBERING
THE TOYS OF OUR CHILDHOOD AND THE FADED
FLOWER PATTERNS ON THE RAGS WE USED TO
DRY OUR DISHES."

"YOU DON'T WANT TO LIVE IN ANY MORE
OF A FANTASY WORLD THAN YOU ALREADY DO;
ARMING AGAINST IMAGINARY THREATS AND

PINING OVER NONEXISTENT RELATIONSHIPS AND
LOVES LONG LOST."

"THE WORLD KNOWS WELL HOW TO SANITIZE EVIL,
BUT NOT RID ITSELF OF IT."

"I CAN'T QUITE PUT MY FINGER ON IT, OR MAYBE
IT'S JUST ME—BUT I THINK THERE'S SOMETHING
HINKEY ABOUT AN OLD ORIENTAL COOK IN A
TRADITIONALLY AUTHENTIC CHINESE RESTAURANT
WITH A MISSING JACK RUSSELL TERRIER THAT
ANSWERS TO THE NAME OF STIR-FRY."

"IN THE BATTLE AND CLASH OF FLINT AGAINST
STEEL, FIRE IS BORN AND EVERYONE WINS."

"A FLINTLOCK IS JUST THE EVOLUTION OF FLINT
AND STEEL POISED TO KILL."

"AS PER OUR CONVERSATION DEAR LADY, YOU'RE
TOO YOUNG AND THERE'S NOTHING WE CAN DO
ABOUT IT; HOWEVER, THAT WILL DISSIPATE WITH
AGE AND BECOME LESS NOTICEABLE WITH TIME ...
SO HANG IN THERE KID."

"WE CAN'T DWELL ON PAIN IN THIS LIFE,
BUT PAIN IS FREE TO DWELL IN US."

"IN LIFE IF YOU HOLD IT STRAIGHT AND CUT IT
STRAIGHT ... IT'LL BE STRAIGHT."

"It's hard to walk away from money no matter how much it's robbing you of."

"One must be as courageous in the face of life, as that of death."

"Fantasy does become reality if enough people buy into it."

"Being scathed in this life is the price you pay for thinking you can get through it unscathed."

"My family and friends love it when I bring fake crab pasta salad to a barbeque or picnic; the crab's real enough, but the salad's fake."

"It's been said that—'you can't legislate morality,' and I quite agree—
but you can and must legislate the framework to support it."

"Like my old granddaddy used to say:
'Rehydration starts with the first drink boy—and there's times when being hydrated is much more important than being sober.'"

"Yes—I'm quite certain that after they left their vaporized bodies, all 19 September 11th Hijackers went straight to hell in gasoline suits, and they haven't stopped screaming yet."

"'If' you can lose your salvation, then in
this life you'll never be free.'
Insight courtesy of Janice Joplin,
from—*Bobby Magee*"

"Christians not only eat of the Kings food—
we eat at the King's table."

"Refreshing honesty in politics: 'Vote for
me and feel free to jump on my bandwagon—
because in this present field of candidates,
I am currently the least repugnant skunk
that's not spraying in your direction.'"

"God plays into our wheelhouse that we
might play into His Wheelhouse."

"Hell, like evil,
will never just burn itself out."

"9-11 is where the world will be at
to the very end."

"One may die in peace and
never rest in peace."

"You know you're not in Heaven if the cry of
your heart is 'More!'"

"Sometimes the man a thief picks to rob
at random turns out to be the wrong
random man."

"ALL WE HUMAN BEINGS HAVE THE ABILITY TO KILL BUT NOT ALL ARE KILLERS; KILLERS ARE KILLERS BEFORE THEY KILL."

"DO IT BECAUSE IT'S WORTH IT; EVEN IF YOU HAVE TO DRAG YOURSELF KICKING AND SCREAMING ALL THE WAY TO DOING THE NEXT RIGHT THING."

"MIND-NUMBING DRUDGERY INFUSED WITH INCOMPETENCE MORPHING INTO INSTANT AND OVERWHELMING CHAOS WHICH WILL NEVER BE ACCOUNTED FOR, SOUNDS LIKE MY CURRENT JOB DESCRIPTION."

"CRYPTIC IS A POLITICIAN'S NATIVE TONGUE—AND VAGARY THEIR SECOND LANGUAGE."

"I MUST BE AT WORK ... BECAUSE I'VE ONLY BEEN HERE FOR AN HOUR AND IT FEELS LIKE THIRTY YEARS."

"PEOPLE IN THESE DAYS OF MODERNITY; BOUND TO ONE ANOTHER BY WHIMSY; CONTINUOUSLY TETHERED WITH DEVICES IN HAND, HAVE REDUCED THEMSELVES TO "COMMUNICATING" IN INCESSANT FLURRIES AND FISTFULS OF INANE AND POORLY CHOSEN ALMOST WORDS."

"WHEN YOU'RE HIGH YOU THINK YOU'RE BEING CREATIVE, BUT YOU'RE JUST BEING HIGH."

"My father was a butcher from a young and early age, so I know the life of a meat-cutter is one of <u>knives kept sharp</u>."

"You really want to solve the problems in your life, not merely alleviate the pain of them."

"Life is pain in the process of mitigation."

"I'm who you think I am;
I'm just not what you think I am."

"Absolutely oblivious; very much <u>unlike</u> our ancestors and a phenomenon of our devices, modern humans no longer look up with awareness, nor around with awe or concern, but always down with distraction."

"We have power ceded to defend our lives, but only provisional power to retain them."

"Once administered, sodium pentothal is a drug that allows you to walk down someone else's memory lane uninvited."

"Seek to be pain free and don't get in the habit of trading one pain for another."

"What in the world is going on is that God is herding a frenetic Humanity toward a reckoning."

"I PRAY THE YESTERDAY WILL COME,
WHEN I LOST THE CARES THAT FRETTED ME."

"SOMETIMES YOU CAN'T REMEMBER IT BECAUSE
IT NEVER HAPPENED."

"YOU NEVER KNOW WHAT A DAY MAY BRING,
OR AN ACT OF KINDNESS OR BRUTALITY MIGHT
ENGENDER."

"GOD HAS IMBEDDED HIMSELF IN HUMANITY AND
THEREFORE WANTS US ALL TO BE INVOLVED IN THE
LIVES OF ... 'THE OTHERS.'"

"SELF-DRIVING 'SMART CARS' WILL NEVER BE
ABLE TO SAVE 'THE DISTRACTED' FROM THEIR
LAZINESS, SELFISHNESS, INCOMPETENCE AND
IGNORANCE ... AND OH YAH ... 'ACCIDENTS.'"

"YAH I FEEL LIKE I'M ON THE SAME PAGE,
BUT I MIGHT BE IN THE WRONG BOOK."

"IF ANYONE HAS EVER WANTED ANYTHING,
<u>NOW</u> IS THE TIME TO GET IT."

"WHY IS IT THAT SOME PEOPLE ARE ADAMANT
ABOUT ADDING NOTHING MORE TO THE
EXPERIENCE AND QUALITY OF YOUR LIFE THAN THE
ENVELOPING ANNOYANCE OF THEIR PRESENCE?"

"NO OF COURSE I WOULDN'T WANT TO BE IN
'THEIR' SHOES! ... THAT'S WHY I'M IN MY SHOES.'"

"SOME COUPLES HAVE AN INTIMATE RECIPROCAL RELATIONSHIP REMINISCENT OF A FLYING ROCK AND A PICTURE WINDOW."

"VISION AND LIGHT MAKE ONE ANOTHER POSSIBLE."

"'IF YOU WANT PEACE, <u>PREPARE FOR WAR;</u>' IF YOU WANT WAR ... DO THE SAME."

"MICE, UNLIKE MEN, DON'T COME-A-RUNNIN' WHEN THEY HEAR THE CRIES OF ONE OF THEIR OWN CAUGHT IN A TRAP."

"IF YOU WANT TO SUCCEED IN LIFE AND BE ABLE TO FOCUS, YOU'LL WANT TO STRIVE TO MAINTAIN A DIET THAT'S HIGH IN FIBER AND LOW IN CLUTTER."

"AN ANALOG WATCH WITH BLACK HANDS AND A BLACK DIAL IS DESIGNED FOR PEOPLE WHO REALLY DON'T WANT TO KNOW WHAT TIME IT IS."

"A PESSIMIST NEVER FEEDS THE BIRDS BECAUSE HE KNOWS THEY'LL JUST CONVERT IT INTO GUANO AND IT'LL END-UP PEPPERING HIS BRAND-NEW CAR—AND AN OPTIMIST FEEDS THEM BECAUSE HE BELIEVES IT'LL ALL BE DROPPED ON THE NEW CAR OF HIS JACKASS NEIGHBOR ACROSS THE STREET."

"THE FULFILLMENT OF OUR HOPES, DREAMS AND HEART'S DESIRES DON'T HAPPEN IN OUR YESTERDAYS, THEY HAPPEN IN OUR TOMORROWS."

"I'D MUCH PREFER HAVING A WOMAN THAT'S
BUILT LIKE A BRICK SHITHOUSE,
THAN A SHIT-BRICK-HOUSE."

"OFTEN TIMES THOSE WHO KEEP STIRRING THE
POT DO SO TO KEEP IT AND US FROM BURNING."

"AIN'T NO REASON TO LIGHT A FIRE IF YOU AIN'T
GOT NOTHIN' TA BURN."

"I'M GENERALLY VERY FRUGAL AND
CONSERVATIVE IN MY SPENDING, BUT I FAR
TOO OFTEN FIND MYSELF STRAINING OUT THE
GNATS, JUST TO MAKE ROOM ENOUGH TO
SWALLOW THE CAMELS."

"SOME PEOPLE ARE 'LIVING THE DREAM;' THE
REST OF US ARE JUST DREAMING ABOUT THE LIFE."

"LIKE MY OLD GRANDDADDY USE TO SAY,
'IF'EN GOD WANTS YOU TA FIND SOMETHIN',
HE AIN'T GONNA PUT IT WHERE YOU AIN'T
LOOKIN'.'"

"MAINTAINING SELF-CONTROL AND RESISTING SIN
DOESN'T HAVE TO BE ELEGANT, ONLY EFFECTIVE."

"IN MODERN AERIAL WARFARE 'MASTERS OF
DISGUISE' ARE INDEED 'MASTERS OF DA SKIES.'"

"A WARDROBE IS AN ITEM FOR THOSE WHO HAVE
TOO MUCH MONEY TO MERELY AFFORD CLOTHES."

"WHEN YOU'RE INVITED TO A BARBECUE OR
PICNIC, DON'T BE THE GUY WHO <u>ALWAYS</u> BRINGS
THE ICE AND NAPKINS."

"I'M A LOT SMARTER THAN I LOOK IN
CERTAIN LIGHT."

"THEY ASKED ME: 'HOW OLD ARE YOU?' I SAID,
'TOO OLD.' THEY SAID, 'HOW COME?'
I SAID, 'BECAUSE I REFUSED TO DIE YOUNG.'"

"THE REASON THEY'RE EVENTUALLY CAUGHT IS
BECAUSE PEOPLE WHO ARE PROUD OF THEIR SINS
NEVER DELETE THEM."

"THE MOST IMPORTANT PART OF A CHURCH IS NOT
THE CROSS ADORNING ITS STEEPLE NOR THE
WEIGHT OF ITS GOLD ... BUT ITS DOORS."

"ONE CAN'T PAY FOR THEIR SINS INDIVIDUALLY,
NOR CAN HUMANITY COLLECTIVELY,
BUT GOD ONLY CAN PAY FOR THEM PERSONALLY."

"EXISTENCE WITHOUT HOPE IS NOT LIFE, BUT THE
STUFF THAT HELL IS MADE OF."

"IF YOU'VE EVER WANTED TO SEE A GROWN MAN
BREAKDOWN AND CRY, THIS IS THE PLACE TO DO
IT; THEY'RE STILL HIRING, THE PAYS GOOD—AND
YOU CAN FEEL FREE TO USE ME AS A REFERENCE."

"MY POLICY IS TO SHINE THE LIGHT INTO THE
DARKNESS, SO WHEN THE GANG-BANGERS AND
THUGS ARE SKULKING AND SHUFFLING THE

STREETS IN THE DEAD OF NIGHT, THEY DON'T 'INADVERTENTLY' STUMBLE AND FALL."

"GOD IS THE AUTHOR OF LIFE,
AND WE ARE BUT HIS CHARACTERS."

"ONE'S HEART MUST BE OPEN FOR LOVE TO FLOW
IN THAT IT MIGHT FLOW OUT."

"COVETED COMFORT IS THE MOST ELUSIVE ZONE
TO MAINTAIN IN ONE'S LIFE."

"I'M NOT TOO YOUNG TO RETIRE;
I'M TOO YOUNG TO STAY."

"SAFETY FIRST, YES, AND REMEMBER YOU'RE
ALWAYS SAFER KEEPING IN THE LORD'S LOOP
THAN MERELY KEEPING THE LORD IN YOURS."

"OFTEN GOD PREPARES US FOR PAIN BY
ALLOWING US PAIN."

"THE PROBLEM WITH LIVING LIFE SO FAST IS THAT
THE ANSWERS TO PROBLEMS COME SLOW."

"WHOMEVER OR WHATEVER YOU MAKE YOUR
ENEMY ... WILL BE."

"HUMAN NATURE AND HISTORY PROVE THAT
NOTHING IS EVER SETTLED BY VIOLENCE—AND AT
BEST, ONLY POSTPONED."

"THE DEAD CAN'T BE HELPED BY THE LIVING,
OR THE LIVING BY THE DEAD."

"HUMANITY IS A DRIVEN RACE WITH DEATH AS THE
FINAL DISTRACTION."

"CONCEPTION AND BIRTH ARE SO UBIQUITOUS:
LIFE SO ETHEREAL; PULLING A TRIGGER SO FINAL."

"GIVEN AN OPPORTUNITY WE ALL BUY A LIFE,
FOR BETTER OR FOR WORSE."

"I'D RATHER BE A TATTOOIST RUNNING OUT OF INK
THAN A TATTOOEE RUNNING OUT OF SKIN."

"A CUTTING TOOL TOO SHARP IS LIKE WATER
THAT'S TOO WET."

"DUE TO SOCIAL MEDIA AND TECHNOLOGY, OUR
MODERN HUMANITY OF OBLIVION HAS REDUCED
ITSELF TO A VAPID AND DISTRACTED CONJOINED
TWIN WITH EYE STRAIN AND DEFT THUMBS."

"I DON'T NEED AN EASY WAY TO MAKE A LIVING;
I WANT A CREATIVE, CHALLENGING AND
PROFITABLE WAY TO DO SO."

"IF THE HANDWRITING IS ALREADY ON THE WALL,
THERE'S NO PRAYING AGAINST IT."

"FOR HUMANITY BEFORE THE GATHERING BEST,
THE WINNOWING WORST IS YET TO COME."

"WHOSE GENERATION IS THE 'ME' GENERATION;
IS IT ... 'MINE?'"

"TALK ABOUT AN ETHNIC MELTING POT OF
ACCOMMODATION WITH NO ASSIMILATION;
MY NEIGHBORHOOD REEKS OF ETHNOS."

"ADDRESSING MY SUBORDINATES I OPINE:
DON'T TELL ME WHAT YOU <u>COULD DO</u>;
TELL ME WHAT YOU <u>DID DO</u> THAT SHOULD
HAVE BEEN DONE."

"IT'S NEVER TOO LATE TO PRAY TO A GOD WHO
CAN RAISE THE DEAD."

"I TOLD MY GUYS: 'KEEP DOING WHAT YOU DO
BEST—AND WHEN YOU'RE FINISHED WITH THAT,
SEE IF YOU CAN GET SOME WORK DONE.'"

"WE'RE ALL DEAD MEN WALKING;
THE QUESTION IS ... TO WHERE?"

"BLEEDING HEARTS AND LIBERALS ARE THOSE
WHO WOULD RATHER GIVE A MAN ONE OF <u>YOUR</u>
FISH, THAN TEACH HIM WHERE AND HOW TO FISH
FOR HIMSELF—AND INSIST THEREAFTER, HE BE
COMPELLED TO DO SO."

"IN THIS LIFE IT'S USUALLY THE DAY 'THE BAG'
BREAKS THAT YOU START DOUBLE-BAGGING."

"IF THE MORAL BREAKS IN YOUR LIFE ARE
SLIPPING AND SQUEAKING,
IT DOESN'T MEAN THEY NEED GREASE."

"You can't stay true to yourself if you're
not trustworthy."

"The big cats hunt and do their best work
when they're hungry."

"The question is asked: 'How many
Christians throughout history died waiting
for the Lord to return and He never did?' …
Not as many as will be waiting for Him at
that time when He does."

"If I need to have my heart broken, let God
be the One to break it, because He's the
only one who knows how to fix it."

"The worst last meal you could ever have
before you die, would be the one where the
shark is eating you."

"Confucius during the Shang Dynasty
(1600-1046 B.C.), insisted and taught that
chopsticks and not knives be used at the
table when eating, because knives were
equated with acts of aggression—and
because Confucius always preferred to
kill his enemies at the table with
chopsticks rather than a knife."

"I make no apologies for being attracted to
women who are attractive to me
and attracted to me."

"WE MODERN HUMANS HAVE DISCONNECTED OURSELVES FROM FACE TO FACE AND EYE TO EYE HUMAN CONTACT AND COMMUNICATION, AND WE ARE NOW BEARING THE FULL WEIGHT OF OUR FAUX RELATIONSHIPS TETHERED TO ONE ANOTHER WITH GOSSAMER CELLULAR THREADS."

"I NO LONGER CARE TO BE PAID FOR MY TIME, BUT MY TALENT."

"IN THIS LIFE EVIL DOESN'T KEEP COMING BACK; IT NEVER LEAVES."

"LIFE ITSELF IS DEATH BY A THOUSAND CUTS."

"ONLY A PERFECT BEING CAN UNDERSTAND AND APPRECIATE PERFECTION."

"THE EMPIRICAL EVIDENCE WILL ONE DAY PROVE, NOT TO HAVE BEEN."

"IT WOULDN'T DO TO ASK HOW THE POOR GOT THERE, BUT HOW TO GET THEM OUT."

"SIN HASN'T CHANGED HEAVEN NOR DIMINISHED HELL."

"GOD HAS MADE IT THUS THAT ONLY A CHRISTIAN CAN SURVIVE DEATH."

"GIVE A MAN A FISH HE'LL EAT FOR A DAY; GIVE HIM A FISH EVERY DAY, AND HE'LL EVENTUALLY WANT STEAK AND LOBSTER."

"You run the extra mile after you've run the first five; not before."

"Killing like death is in the DNA of humanity and will be until death is no longer possible."

"I like foods and drink that get the taste of defeat out of my mouth."

"I never get involved in violence, but if I ever do get involved, it's going to turn-out very badly for those who got me involved."

"September 11th caused the 'sleeping giant' to flail for a season, and then forgetting 'the price of liberty,' to roll over and continue his slumber."

"Unfailing abundance engenders a forgetfulness of needful things, while want for a lack of bread makes one learn to be thankful when it comes."

"The new normal in America referred to as 'freedom,' has gotten to be doing whatever anyone wants to do, until and unless somebody stops them."

"Intellect isn't keeping-up with our technology, and the only 'reality' we're escaping to on our devices is the one we've already created in our collective consciousness."

"AMERICA HAS ALREADY CROSSED THE RUBICON, AND HER FEET ARE NOW DRY AND PLANTED ON THE OTHER SIDE."

"I CRITICIZE AMERICA FOR THE SAME REASON A WRITER KEEPS EDITING HIS WORK— BECAUSE I WANT IT TO BE THE VERY BEST THAT IT CAN BE."

"THE BROKEN PEACE ONCE REESTABLISHED, CAN NEVER JUSTIFY OR AMELIORATE THE HORRORS OF WAR WHICH PRECEDED IT—AND WILL ALWAYS AND IRREVOCABLY DIMINISH OUR HUMANITY AND OBLITERATE ANY ALTERNATE FUTURE THAT MIGHT HAVE BEEN."

"AS A WRITER, I DO LOVE LOSING MYSELF IN A PUZZLE OF ARRANGING WORDS AND COMING OUT THE MAZE ON THE OTHER SIDE UNSCATHED."

"IF ONE FIRST ENCOUNTERS AND EMBRACES THE GENUINE ARTICLE; ONE NEED NOT CONTINUE TO INVESTIGATE THE COUNTERFEITS."

"NOTHING COMES AFTER 'THE END,' OR IT WOULDN'T BE THE END, BUT MAYBE THERE IS NO END—AND IF NOT...?"

"BE IT BY FRIEND OR FOE, SOMETIMES YOUR GREATEST ASSET IS BEING UNDERESTIMATED."

"YES, GOD IS ALIVE, BUT SATAN IS AFOOT."

"I DON'T NEED THE WIND AT MY BACK;
I JUST DON'T WANT IT IN MY FACE."

"SUCCESS IS THE CATALYST FOR SUCCESS,
BECAUSE FAILURE IS NONADDICTIVE."

"THE VAST MAJORITY OF POISON HUMANITY
INGESTS IS ADMINISTERED THROUGH THE EYES
AND EARS."

"THEY ASKED ME AND SAID: 'IF YOU DON'T BELIEVE
THAT EVERYTHING YOU WRITE IS TRUE, WHY THEN
DO YOU WRITE IT?' ...AND I OPINE: 'BECAUSE
THERE'S ALWAYS A CHANCE I MIGHT BE WRONG.'"

"THE QUESTION DOESN'T OFTEN COME UP,
BUT IN MY OPINION, A PERSON WHO'S AN EXPERT
IN INEXPERIENCE, IS A NOVICE."

"IT'S NEVER BEEN ABOUT QUALITY, INTEGRITY OR
INVENTORY; IT'S ALWAYS BEEN ABOUT CONNING
THE BUCKWHEATS, THE HAYSEEDS AND THE
HUCKLEBERRIES I OPINE ... AND IF THE COMBAT
BOOTS ARE FALLING OFF THE FEET OF THE
INFANTRY SOLDIERS WHILE THEY'RE MARCHING,
IT'S BECAUSE THEY WERE MADE AND MEANT FOR
THE CAVALRY."

"IT'S A GOOD THING THAT I RETIRED, BECAUSE IF I
DIDN'T, I WOULDN'T BE GETTING ANYTHING DONE."

"THE DEAD CAN'T SPEAK TO US FROM BEYOND THE
GRAVE, BUT DEATH ITSELF DOES."

"WE'RE A BLEAK RACE, RUNNING A BLEAK RACE—
AND ULTIMATELY THE ONLY THING THAT WILL BIND
HUMANITY TOGETHER IN THE VERY END …
IS OUR COLLECTIVE PAIN."

"BOTOX® IS THE BACTERIAL TOXIN <u>BOTULIN</u>;
ONE OF THE USES OF WHICH IS
THE REHYDRATION OF 'OLD TURDS.'"

"EVEN IF YOU HAVE TO GO BACK TO FIND WHAT
PRECIOUS THING YOU'VE LOST,
YOU'RE NEVER LOSING GROUND AND YOU'RE STILL
MOVING FORWARD."

"GIRLS, YOU'LL BE WISE TO SHY AWAY FROM THE
BOY IN HIGH SCHOOL WHO WAS UNANIMOUSLY
VOTED: 'THE GUY MOST LIKELY TO BUY A PANEL
VAN WITH NO WINDOWS JUST AS SOON AS HE
GRADUATES.'"

"I LIVE BY THE OLD ADAGE: 'AN OUNCE OF
INTENTION IS WORTH A POUND OF MANURE.' …
'SO JUST DO IT! —SLACK-WAD!'"

"GOD DIDN'T CREATE A CLAW-AND-FANG; DOG-EAT-
DOG WORLD OF DEATH AND CORRUPTION—
SIN AND HUMAN NATURE HAS MADE IT THUS."

"RETIREMENT ISN'T A DAY, NOR AN EVENT, OR THE
END OF THE LAST HOUR ON THE CLOCK, BUT A
SEGUE; A CONTINUING OF THE SEAMLESS PROCESS
OF TRANSITION FROM YOUR PAST LIFE TO THAT OF
THE FUTURE, AND A NEW SONG OR STORY WHICH
MAY YET NEED TO BE WRITTEN BY YOU."

"IT QUALIFIES AS AN OBSERVATION IF YOU THINK IT MIGHT NOT BE TRUE; IT BECOMES A JUDGMENT IF YOU BELIEVE IT IS."

"IF YOU GET IN THE HABIT OF USING WHISKY FOR GUTS TO SEE YOU THROUGH THE DIRE STRAITS, ONE DAY THE WILY AND CLEARHEADED ON THE OTHER SIDE WILL BE USING YOUR GUTS FOR GARTERS."

"IT'S HARD TO CHALLENGE THE THINKING OF PEOPLE WHO ARE NOT THINKING PEOPLE."

"BE CAREFUL, BECAUSE SOMETIMES WHEN YOU SEEK TO REMOVE THEIR SHARP EDGES, PEOPLE LIKE THINGS CAN BECOME DULL."

"SATAN DOESN'T HAVE TO DO MUCH TO COMPEL HUMANITY TO DO WHAT COMES NATURAL; ONLY GREASE THE SKIDS FROM TIME TO TIME."

["AH FOR THE GOOD OLD DAYS"]
"ACTUALLY SIR, I DO HAPPEN TO KNOW THE NAME OF THE ... 'NUTTIER-N-A SQUIRREL TURD EINSTEIN WANNA BE LEADER OF IRAN, WHO WANTS-TA SPLIT THE ATOM AND BUST A NUCLEAR CAP IN AMERICA'S ASS, GOT EYES LIKE A COUPLE OF PISS HOLES IN THE MUD, HAS SHORTNESS OF HEIGHT, DON'T WEAR NO TIE AND LOOKS LIKE HE COMBS HIS HAIR WITH A GREASY PORK CHOP'—AND I'M QUITE CERTAIN IT'S PRONOUNCED ... *AH-MA-DIN-E-JAD*, NOT, ABBA-JABBA-JIB-A-JAB MR. PRESIDENT."
—CONDI RICE

"EVERYONE WANTS A PIECE OF YOU BECAUSE YOU'RE OF INFINITE VALUE, BUT ONLY AS LONG AS YOU'RE A PAYING COSTUMER."

"WHEN YOU ENTER THE RACE THAT IS HUMAN, NEVER DECIDE BEFOREHAND HOW FAR YOU'RE WILLING TO GO BEFORE YOU QUIT RUNNING."

"THERE IS NO PURGATORY; ONLY HEAVEN AND HELL AND A BATTLEFIELD CALLED EARTH."

"WE'RE ALL DYING; FOR SOME OF US IT'S JUST IN SLOWER MOTION THAN OTHERS."

"PARSLEY ALONE WON'T DO FOR THE CLAM CHOWDER, AND I'M REALLY IN QUITE A BIT OF A RUSH, THOUGH I FOUND SOME SAGE AND ROSEMARY, BUT I STILL LACK THE THYME."

"EVEN THE MOST COSTLY AND PRECIOUS DIAMOND PLATINUM OR GOLD RING LOSES ITS BEAUTY APPEAL AND LUSTER, WHEN VIEWED ADORNING ONE'S VERY OWN, OLD, BONY AND WIZENED FINGER."

"SATAN AND HIS DEMONS CAN'T READ YOUR MIND, BUT THEY LOVE TO PERUSE OUR HUMAN NATURE— AND THEN TROLL."

"MY LORD BUT ONCE DESIRED AND REQUIRED SACRIFICE OF HIMSELF—AND OF HIS CHILDREN ... 'MERCY.'"

"Beware; the truth can offend more thoroughly than lies."

"'Please wait!' is getting to be the story of our modern lives."

"When the reckoning comes, entire nations as surely as individual men, will not find themselves in that day more harshly judged for how low and loathsome they know themselves to be, but for how far from the hand of Grace <u>they've chosen to fall</u> to get there."

"Once you sharpen a knife don't go playing with it, or you might just prove it.

"The song '<u>This Land Was Made for You and Me</u>' was once quite popular in the folk music communities of the U.S. in the 1940s & 50s, but I've noticed it never really caught on with '<u>this land's</u>' Native Americans."

"Don't fall for it, because <u>in this life</u>, 'It's too late!' ... is just a trick of the devil."

"In this current global dynamic maybe those troubled by it are the only ones who are normal."

"Humanity at Armageddon will prove that puppets will continue to dance until they have their cords cut."

"God is absolutely sovereign and perfectly just—and may say to one man, 'Sell all that you have and give the proceeds to the poor,' and to the man standing next to him … 'I want you to buy up everything that guy will be selling.'"

"The attitude of too many has gotten to be … 'Here I am; do something about me.'"

"I recently acquired a partial hearing loss in my left ear, but I'm not overly concerned about it, and in fact, I count it a blessing, because it's the ear that the Devil used to whisper into."

"A man's gifting and strengths can be increased or diminished significantly depending on where, if, and how he chooses to use them."

"I love it when it gets to the point in the process where I can say—'All right! … 'Finally!' … 'We're <u>not</u> gettin' <u>nowhere</u> fast!'"

"I'm a Christian because it's the only way to go … and the only way to get there."

"I don't believe in omens, but in God's providence and promise, that His children, and those not so inclined, will in this life, experience and be witness to both good and evil."

"I'M NOTHING IF NOT BRILLIANT—AND OF COURSE
... MODEST."

"LIFE IS SO CHEAP ON PLANET EARTH BECAUSE
IT'S A GIFT THAT HAS COST US NOTHING."

"SOMETIMES THE WICKED DON'T GO TO HELL IN
WHAT SOME MIGHT DEEM A TIMELY FASHION,
BUT RATHER, HELL COMES TO MEET THEM IN THIS
LIFE ... HERE AND NOW."

"THE MEASURE OF A MAN IS GOD'S JUDGMENT,
NOT THE WORLD'S OPINION."

"IF YOU <u>ACHIEVE VICTORY</u> WAR WILL RETURN, IF
YOU <u>ATTAIN PEACE</u> WAR WILL CEASE."

"WHEN ONE COMES TO SPIRITUAL WARFARE, YOU
MUST NEVER GIVE UP AND ALWAYS ENDEAVOR TO
PERSEVERE, BECAUSE WHEN YOU THINK YOU
MIGHT BE LOSING IT, YOU MAY VERY WELL BE ON
THE VERY CUSP OF FINDING IT, AND THEREIN ...
LIES YOUR VICTORY."

"LIFE IN LARGE PART IS A PROCESS OF MITIGATING
THE CONSEQUENCES OF 'OTHER PEOPLE' DOING
THE WRONG THING, AND <u>WE ALL OF US</u>, TO
SOMEONE OUT THERE, <u>ARE</u> THOSE VERY PEOPLE,
WHO ARE DOING THE WRONG THING."

"WHEN IT COMES TO DEALING WITH THE TOUGH
NUT OF PARENTING, SOMETIMES WHEN YOU OVER-
TIGHTEN IT, IT'LL LEAK MORE, THAN IF YOU JUST
LEFT IT ALONE."

"We all have much more to offer this world than merely our time on the clock, and then ... retiring from it."

"Sometimes the only thing holding you back is that there's nothing immediate for you to move forward to."

"Human beings don't want to be free; we just want to be able to choose our own masters."

"America has abandoned her faith in all but self, alongside the road she travels toward a nebulous future."

"I may not have gotten very far in this life, but I've sure come a long way to get here."

"It's worse and more complicated than you think; when you come to the fork in the road you have <u>four</u> possible choices to make; when you come to the crossroads ... you've got <u>five</u>."

"If the challenges in our lives came conveniently in a timely fashion and with plenty of 'heads-up,' they wouldn't be challenges now would they ... and what fun would that be?"

"God only knows the horrific sacrifices made on behalf of humanity by those heroic souls unknown to all but Him."

"IF IN THE BLACKJACK OF LIFE ITSELF, YOU FIND YOURSELF LOOSING BIG, THERE'S NO POINT IN CALLING THE DEALER AN IDIOT."

"IT SEEMS THE MORE POPULAR YOU BECOME TO THE WORLD, THE LESS POPULAR JESUS THE CHRIST BECOMES WITH YOU."

"IN THIS MODERN WORLD OF INSTANT AND CONTINUOUS COMMUNICATION, UP IS WHERE THE ANSWER IS COMING FROM, AND EVERYONE IS LOOKING DOWN."

"WELL YOU'VE GOT ME THERE MY YOUNG FRIEND; I HAVE GOTTEN OLD, BUT THAT'S JUST BECAUSE AT THE TIME IT WAS THE ONLY ALTERNATIVE I HAD TO DYING YOUNG."

"HOPE SPRINGS ETERNAL, BUT TOO OFTEN KEEPS BEING DRAWN BY MOST OF HUMANITY FROM THE SAME SOUR SPRING."

"IF YOU GROW A BEARD OR DO YOUR OWN SHAVING AND HAIRCUTTING, YOU'LL NEVER BE AT THE MERCY OF A BARBER; IF YOU TAKE GOOD CARE OF YOUR PHYSICAL AND MENTAL HEALTH, YOU'LL NEVER BE AT THE MERCY OF A DOCTOR, DENTIST OR SHRINK; IF YOU'RE WISE WITH YOUR FINANCES, YOU'LL NEVER BE A THE MERCY OF A BANKER, STOCK BROKERS OR LOAN SHARKS, AND IF YOU BECOME AN ATHEIST TO BOOT, YOU'LL STILL BE HOWEVER, AT THE MERCY OF THE LIVING GOD."

"YOU, ME, WE ALL OF US HUMAN BEINGS, HAVE THE INCREDIBLE ABILITY IN THE GYMNASTICS

OF OUR OWN MINDS, TO JUSTIFY OURSELVES AND OUR MOTIVES EVEN IN THE MIDST OF OUR MOST BITTER REPENTANCE AND LAVISH SELF-DEPRECATION."

"REMEMBER THAT IT'S ALWAYS 9/11 FOR SOMEONE SOMEWHERE, AND MOST HEROES ARE THOSE UNSUNG."

"'HOPE SPRINGS ETERNAL,' 'THERE'S A SUCKER BORN EVERY MINUTE,' AND THEREFORE … 'A FOOL AND HIS MONEY ARE SOON PARTED.'"

"THE HEART WANTS WHAT IT WANTS, ONCE IT KNOWS WHAT IT WANTS."

"IN THE GAME OF LIFE FOR A CHRISTIAN, IT DOESN'T MATTER IF YOU HAVE A SMALL PART TO PLAY, AS LONG AS YOU HAVE A BIG NAME BACKING YOU."

"A LITTLE MEAT ON THE BONES, AND A LITTLE JUNK IN THE TRUNK IS WHAT MAKES THE WORLD-GO-ROUND."

"THE COLOR OF THE SKIN DOES NOT ESTABLISH OR NEGATE ONE'S CHARACTER, NOR JUSTIFY ONE'S BAD BEHAVIOR."

"IF YOU HOLD YOURSELF AND OTHERS TO VERY LOW STANDARDS, YOU'LL RARELY BE DISAPPOINTED."

"I BELIEVE IN THE POWER OF PRAYERS AS
THOROUGHLY AS IN GOD'S SOVEREIGNTY
AND DISCRETION IN ANSWERING THEM."

"VERY LITTLE OF TRUE QUALITY AND
VALUE IS PRODUCED THESE DAYS …
'BUT WE MAKE LOTS-OF-IT!'"

"DON'T WALK AWAY FROM PRAYER UNTIL
YOU DO SO WITH AN ANSWER."

"THOSE WHO ACCOMPLISH SOMETHING GREAT,
ALWAYS SACRIFICE SOMETHING GREAT."

"THERE'S NEVER A 'QUICK AND EASY' ANSWER,
BECAUSE QUICK AND EASY DON'T SOLVE THE
PROBLEMS, AND AT BEST, ONLY TEMPORARILY
AMELIORATE THE AGONY."

"I DON'T THINK THEY SHOULD MAKE DRUGS LEGAL,
I THINK 'THEY,' SHOULD <u>MAKE WORK
MANDATORY</u>."

"I'VE NOTICED THAT MOST PEOPLE'S DOGS HAVE
THEM PRETTY WELL TRAINED."

"IF AT FIRST YOU DON'T SUCCEED, ASK YOUR
PAROLE OFFICER—'WHY?'"

"THE TRUTH CAN BE DENIED OR MITIGATED,
BUT NEVER DESTROYED."

"IF YOU DON'T <u>HAVE TO BE</u> ANYWHERE;
YOU <u>CAN BE</u>, ANYWHERE YOU ARE."

"IT'S EASIER TO BE ACCOUNTABLE WHEN YOU'RE
HELD TO ACCOUNT, RATHER THAN WHEN YOU'RE
GIVEN FREE REIGN TO POLICE YOURSELF."

"IN MY DREAMS I'M ALWAYS A HERO ... IF ONLY THE
HERO COULD ESCAPE FROM MY DREAMS."

"I FIND YOU'RE BETTER OFF KNOWING EVERYTHING
THERE IS TO KNOW ABOUT NOTHING,
THAN KNOWING NOTHING AT ALL ABOUT
ANYTHING."

"ALL GOD'S CREATURES DIE IN WARS, ESPECIALLY
THOSE CREATED IN HIS IMAGE WHO START THEM."

"SOME FEW PEOPLE ACTUALLY HAVE A
PHOTOGRAPHIC, I.E. EIDETIC MEMORY;
WHILE OTHERS MERELY HAVE ONE THAT'S
KLEPTOMANIACAL."

"WHEN I'VE GOT NOTHING MORE TO SAY, YOU'LL
BE THE FIRST TO HEAR FROM ME."

"BETTER THAT YOU SHOULD CURSE THE DULL
KNIFE YOU'RE USING, THAN CUT YOUR FINGER TO
THE BONE CAVALIERLY WIELDING ONE THAT'S SKIN
CRAWLINGLY SHARP ... 'JUST SAYIN.'"

"REGARDING THE DREADFUL MORASS I PERCEIVE
THE WORLD SLIPPING INTO, I DON'T THINK IT'S

BECAUSE HUMAN NATURE HAS CHANGED, I JUST
BELIEVE THAT IT'S NO LONGER SUFFICIENTLY
RESTRAINED."

"GOD HAS PROVEN HIMSELF TO BE THE AUTHOR
OF LIFE; HUMANITY, THE ARCHITECTS AND
ENGINEERS OF DEATH."

"JUST AS ONE MUST PICK THEIR FIGHTS YOU MUST
CAREFULLY CHOOSE YOUR PASSIONS IN THIS LIFE;
FOR SOMETIMES, THEY'RE ONE AND THE SAME."

"IF THE PROHIBITIONISTS COULD'VE BOTTLED
BIBLICAL JOY IN THEIR DAY, ALCOHOL WOULD'VE
BEEN LONG AGO ABOLISHED AND OBSOLETE."

"THE FASTEST GROWING RELIGION IN 'AMERICA
THE LIBERTINE,' ISN'T CHRISTIANITY OR ISLAM,
BUT CRASS CONSUMERISM AND
OVERINDULGENCE."

"PEACE IS NOT AN END IN ITSELF, FOR YOU CAN'T
LONG HAVE PEACE WITHOUT PURPOSE NOR
PURPOSE WITH PEACE DENIED, FOR THEY ARE THE
TWO SIDES OF THE SAME COIN, AND A LIFE OF
PURPOSE IS ONE THAT ATTAINS PEACE, AND A LIFE
OF PEACE ONE THAT ENGENDERS PURPOSE, FOR
PEACE WITHOUT PURPOSE CAN'T LAST, AND
PURPOSE WITHOUT PEACE CAN'T BE SUSTAINED."

"QUIT PISSING AND MOANING AND TRY LOOKING
ON THE BRIGHT SIDE FOR A CHANGE;
AT LEAST YOU'RE NOT A QUADRIPLEGIC MIME WITH
TOURETTE SYNDROME CHAIN-SMOKING LUCKY
STRIKES IN AN OXYGEN TENT."

"WHERE I LIVE, AND IN TOO MANY OTHER VENUES
I'M SURE, FOLKS AND NEIGHBORS GETTING-UP AND
GOING ABOUT THE BUSINESS OF THEIR DAY,
DOESN'T IMPLY GOING TO WORK."

"THE FLAWS ARE ALWAYS ON THE <u>OTHER SIDE</u>
OF THE MASK."

"THE MORE I LEARN ABOUT HUMAN HISTORY AND
NATURE, THE MORE I'VE COME TO REALIZE HOW
WRONG, RAGGEDY-ASS AND FRAGILE WE TRULY
ARE; LIKE A LITTER OF HAPLESS PUPPY-DOGS,
RUNNING AROUND AND PLAYING ON A SIX-LANE
HIGHWAY OBLIVIOUS TO THE ONSLAUGHT OF RUSH
HOUR TRAFFIC."

"I ASKED MY OLD FRIEND WHY AFTER A CAREER
OF FORTY-ONE YEARS HE'S NOT YET RETIRED,
AND HE SAID ... 'BECAUSE THERE ARE STILL
A FEW PEOPLE AROUND HERE I HAVEN'T PISSED-
OFF YET.'"

"HOW MANY TIMES DO YOU HAVE TO DO THINGS
WRONG BEFORE THEY TURN OUT RIGHT? —
HINT, HINT ... 'NEVER.'"

"MODERN HUMANITY IS THE ETERNALLY
OPTIMISTIC POSTER CHILD FOR PUSHING THE
ENVELOPE; A PARAPLEGIC 'RUNNING' IN THE
BOSTON MARATHON THIS YEAR AND WITH THE
BULLS IN PAMPLONA NEXT YEAR."

"SOME PEOPLE LIVE IN A FANTASY WORLD
BECAUSE REALITY IS STRANGER THAN FICTION."

"Does no one any longer ever ask themselves: 'Was I not made for better than this?'"

"I have as much faith in God answering my prayers, as in His sovereignty in doing so."

"Choosing to commit abortion is killing a half of oneself, and half of someone else's self, which always equals one human life."

"Like those of the animal kingdom I don't make threats, but I do give warning."

"Everyone likes a freak because they make us feel better about ourselves, until they become an Einstein, Gates or Hawking."

"Sometimes there are points in time you just want your fellow travelers to get up, hit the road and keep-on movin'."

"Most of my life I've been tired, and if not tired ... weary."

"If those who die with the most toys win; you can be sure that hell will be full of <u>only</u> 'the winners.'"

"Humanity has always been a failing proposition with redemptive flashes of Divine brilliance."

"A 'NEW BROOM' SWEEPS CLEAN BUT ONLY GETS
RID OF WHAT IT DEEMS 'NECESSARY,'
UNTIL A NEWER BROOM SHOWS-UP AND DEEMS IT
NECESSARY ... AND SO IT GOES."

"YOU CAN UNDERSTAND HUMAN HISTORY IF YOU
CAN UNDERSTAND HUMAN NATURE ...
AND THE FUTURE AS WELL."

"INSTANT GRATIFICATION DOESN'T ENRICH YOUR
LIFE AND MAKE YOU A BETTER HUMAN BEING, THE
PROCESS OF PRESSING TOWARD THE MARK AND
ACHIEVING THE GOAL DOES."

"HEED IT OR NOT, BELIEVE IT OR NO;
GOD'S <u>PRIME DIRECTIVE</u> FOR HUMANITY HAS
ALWAYS BEEN: "BE PREPARED FOR, AND GET
READY TO ... <u>LEAVE THIS PLANET</u>."

"YOU CAN NEVER FAIL OR GIVE-UP IF YOU DECIDE
TO BE SOMEONE SIGNIFICANT IN THE LIFE OF
OTHERS, BECAUSE YOU'LL ALWAYS HAVE A LIFE
WORTH LIVING AND SOMEONE TO BE LIVING FOR."

"BE A REGULAR GUY WILL-YA! —AND NEVER MAKE
A TOAST WITH ANYTHING THAT DOESN'T HAVE
'LIFE' IN IT ... THAT IS TO SAY,
<u>PERCENTAGE OF ALCOHOL BY VOLUME</u>."

"IT SEEMS TO BE POPULAR IN THE THEORY OF
MODERN CULTURE TO SAY THAT 'YOU HAVE TO
BE BAD TO BE GOOD.' YOU DON'T—BUT IN TOO
MANY BURGEONING VENUES, YOU HAVE TO BE
BAD TO BE ACCEPTED."

"You can't deceive God because He created the devices we rely on and all the mechanisms we employ."

"In some states the only qualification for getting a medical marijuana card, is being able say '<u>medical marijuana card</u>' clearly, and three times fast, while you're toasted-crispy, or simply spell marijuana correctly while you're straight."

"As soon as <u>the good we choose to do</u> leaves our hand it enters God's ledger and there's nothing more we can do about it, for very much <u>unlike the wrong we've done</u> we can't take it back, and it is fixed to our account forever."

"Does it seem so outlandish and hard to do things right from the very beginning that no one ever even tries anymore?"

"Where I live, we have no sun in winter; only fifty shades of gray dancing across the snow."

"I find myself able to answer too many questions that you don't even know you're asking."

"Don't be afraid to cry, because our God is used to the prayers of humanity being delivered-up to Him on a river of tears."

"I REALLY NEED SOME STRENGTH IN MY LIFE,
BECAUSE WEAKNESS IS GETTING ME
NOWHERE FAST."

"THE MATTER IS TIME SENSITIVE, SO DON'T REMAIN
A THEORETICAL CHRISTIAN FOR TOO LONG."

"A RELATIONSHIP OF LOVE UNREQUITED IS MORE
GRIEVOUS THAN A UNION WITH NO LOVE AT ALL."

"FOR THOSE WHO ARE SUFFERING,
PAIN AND DELIVERANCE ARE NOT THEORETICAL"

"DEAR GIRLS AND FAIR LADIES, JUST A HEADS-UP
TO THE NEOPHYTES AMONG YOU; NO MATTER HOW
DESPERATE YOU BECOME, DON'T GET IN THE HABIT
OF GETTING ALL DOLLED-UP LIKE BAIT AND JUST
PUTTING IT OUT THERE AND TROLLING (TO USE A
FISHING METAPHOR), BECAUSE WHAT YOU PULL IN
ON YOUR LINE AT THE END OF THE DAY, MIGHT NOT
BE THE 'LAKE TROUT, BLUE PIKE, KING SALMON OR
WALLEYE' YOU'RE HOPING FOR, BUT A 'SUCKER,
SHEEP-HEAD, GARPIKE OR CRAPPY,' AND ONCE
YOU'VE GOT THEM FLOPPING AROUND ON YOUR
DECK, THEY'LL STINK-UP YOUR 'BOAT' AND BE A
WHOLE LOT HARDER TO THROW BACK THAN THEY
WERE TO CATCH ... 'JUST SAYIN.'"

"IT'S A FINE LINE TO WALK, BUT IF YOU'RE TOO
IMPETUOUS YOU MAY JUST REGRET WHAT YOU DO,
AND IF YOU DRAG YOUR FEET TOO LONG,
YOU MIGHT REGRET WHAT YOU DIDN'T."

"LIFE IS A PROPOSITION FULL OF TERRIBLE
DECISIONS THAT HAVE TO BE MADE BECAUSE

OF THE POSSIBLE CONSEQUENCES OF THE ALTERNATIVE."

"AMERICA THE ONCE-WELCOMING OF FOREIGNERS AND THOSE OF OTHER CULTURES NO LONGER ACCOMMODATES AND ASSIMILATES; WE NOW EITHER OSTRACIZE OR HOMOGENIZE."

"TO SEE EACH OTHER AS THE 'OTHER,'
WE SEE ONE ANOTHER AS THE ENEMY,
AND ... TREAT THEM ACCORDINGLY."

"'IT WAS OUR SIN THAT ROBBED HUMANITY OF OUR IMMORTALITY AND REBELLION THAT CAST US FROM GLORY, BUT NOT BEYOND THE REACH OF THE HAND OF GRACE."

"TO COMMIT ATROCITY,
ONE MUST DEHUMANIZE THEIR VICTIM;
MUCH AS IN THE CASE OF ABORTION."

"EVENTUALLY EVERYONE CATCHES A 'BULLET' WITH THEIR NAME ON IT."

"CONFUCIUS SAY: 'IF YOUR SUPPER CONSISTS OF ONLY BUTTER-PAN-FRIED LEFTOVER MASHED POTATOES, YOU'VE GOT TO EAT THE WHOLE PAN DUDE—AND DON'T FORGET THE KETCHUP.'"

"MARIJUANA IS A SOCIAL LUBRICANT, BUT ONLY AMONG THOSE WHO ARE LUBRICATED IN THE SAME WAY."

"GOD DOESN'T JUST WANT TO GIVE US WHAT WE WANT; HE WANTS US TO WANT ALL THAT HE'S OFFERING."

"THE DYSFUNCTIONAL, ARE ALWAYS <u>EFFORTLESSLY PREPARING</u> THE NEXT GENERATION FOR A LIFE OF DYSFUNCTION."

"THE PATH OF LEAST RESISTANCE HAS FOREVER BEEN STREWN WITH THE MOLDING HUSKS AND WINDBLOWN CHAFF OF THE LAZY."

"YAH I USED TO BE A BUM ... BUT I'VE RETIRED."

"WHEN ALL IS WELL AND SEEMS RIGHT WITH THE WORLD, WAIT A WHILE LONGER AND SCRATCH A LITTLE DEEPER."

"WHEN EVERYONE IN A SOCIETY IS RUDE, BASE AND HAS POOR SOCIAL SKILLS, THE POINT IS NO LONGER MOOT."

"IT'S NOT THOSE WHO CHALLENGE YOUR THINKING AND COMPEL YOU TO DEFEND YOUR BELIEF SYSTEM THAT ARE THE ENEMY, BUT THEY WHO HAND YOU A FREE PASS ALLOWING YOU TO DECLINE ALL CHALLENGE."

"AN OPTIMIST WOULD BE THE ONE TO SAY: 'I REALLY FEEL GOOD ABOUT OUR CHANCES GUYS— AND I THINK WE'RE GOING TO MAKE IT!' A PESSIMIST IS THE ONE WHO WOULD BE FOUND RUNNING-AROUND FLAILING AND SCREAMING: 'THE PLANE'S GOING DOWN, AND WE'RE ALL GOING TO DIE A HORRIBLE FIERY DEATH!'

A REALIST OR SANGUINE WOULD ASK:
'STEWARDESS, COULD I PLEASE GET A SECOND
OPINION FROM THE COPILOT?'"

"A DEARTH OF SHACKLES DOES NOT A FREE MAN
MAKE, NOR A PLETHORA OF CHAINS A SLAVE."

"THIS IS A METAPHOR OF <u>MY PHILOSOPHY OF LIFE
ITSELF</u>: 'I DON'T DRINK MUCH 'HARD LIQUOR
WHISKEY,' BUT WHEN I DO,
IT'S <u>ALWAYS TOP SHELF</u>."

"OXYCONTIN® <u>IS NOT</u> A DRUG TO BE TAKEN
LIGHTLY—AND IF YOU'VE BEEN PRESCRIBED A
PRESCRIPTION OF FORTY PILLS OR MORE BY YOUR
SURGEON OR PHYSICIAN, AND CHOOSE NOT TO USE
THEM, <u>DON'T</u> JUST THROW THEM AWAY OR FLUSH
THEM, BUT GIVE THEM TO A TRUSTED AND
INTIMATE FRIEND LIKE ME, WHO WILL KNOW
PRECISELY HOW TO DISPOSE OF THEM PROPERLY
IN YOUR BEHALF."

"GOD DOESN'T WANT YOU TO BE CAREFUL SO YOU
DON'T GET CAUGHT, HE WANTS YOU TO BE
RIGHTEOUS SO YOU'RE NOT FOUND GUILTY."

"AS LONG AS WE KEEP TRYING TO SOLVE
HUMANITY'S PROBLEMS WITHOUT GOD AS THE
ALPHA AND THE OMEGA OF THE PERMUTATION;
THE AGGREGATE OF OUR HUMAN WILL AND
INTELLECT SHALL FAIL US."

"I'VE COME TO FIND THAT DISINFORMATION AND
MISUNDERSTANDING IS WHAT MAKES THE WORLD
GO-ROUND."

"I'VE NEVER HAD MUCH OF A LIFE,
BUT I DO FIND THE IDEA INTRIGUING."

I THOUGHT IT WAS JUST IN REAL LIFE …
BUT EVEN IN MY DREAMS THE
PEOPLE ARE WEIRD."

"FEAR IS COMMON, BUT PARALYZING FEAR
YOU HAVE TO CONQUER."

"SOMETIMES THE FIRST 'SHOT' IS JUST A
WARNING SHOT FOR THE NEXT TIME, BECAUSE
ALCOHOL HAS A WAY OF SNEAKING-UP ON YOU
AND GIVING YOU A WARM BOOZY KICK IN THE ASS
JUST AS A PARTING SHOT."

"QUID PRO QUO WON'T CUT IT, BECAUSE THE
DECREED EXCHANGE RATE OF THE HOLY ETERNAL
IS SUCH THAT—ALL THE 'GOOD' WE DO, COULD
NEVER PAY FOR ALL THE EVIL WE'VE DONE."

"YOU'VE GOT ME AS A WITNESS … 'HELLS YAH!'
BECAUSE I CAN SEE CLEARLY THE PROBLEM—
AND I HEAR IT EVERY DAY, ALL DAY AND NIGHT
LONG, AS THEY SLOWLY AND REPEATEDLY ROLL BY
IN THEIR UNAFFORDABLE SUVS AND JALOPIES;
FEASTING AND NOURISHED BY THE 'SOOTHING
BALM' OF THE WORDS OF THEIR PROPHETS;
DRUMMING THROUGH MY NEIGHBORHOOD AND
THEIR SKULLS, IN VULGAR BASE VIBRATION;
SPRAYING FERAL THEIR SUPPOSED TERRITORY
WITH VIBRATING BASE AUDIO-STINK, LIKE A DOG
PISSING ON A FIRE HYDRANT OR TREE THAT THE
LAST HAPLESS MONGREL PISSED ON—AND WITH NO
REDEEMING QUALITY, GOOD PURPOSE OR
RATIONAL REASON FOR US ALL."

"DEATH, GOD NEVER INTENDED, SO IT'S NOT A BODILY FUNCTION, BUT THE FINAL LACK THEREOF."

"STRIVE TO BE LITHE, BECAUSE PUMPING IRON AND BEEFING-UP JUST MAKES YOU A BIGGER AND MORE MUSCLE-BOUND TARGET.

"ONE MUST KEEP THEIR EYES ABOVE THE WAVES TO SEE JESUS, FOR IT'S UPON THE WAVES THAT HE WALKS, AND ON THE WINGS OF THE WIND HE RIDES."

"OFTEN TIMES, THE NEGATIVE THINGS WE'RE WITNESSING AND ARE MADE A PARTY TO IN THE SOCIAL ARENA ARE NOT SOCIAL PROBLEMS AT ALL, BUT SPIRITUAL ISSUES MANIFESTING THEMSELVES SOCIALLY, OR MORE TO THE POINT, ANTISOCIALLY."

"THERE'S NOTHING WRONG WITH BEING IMPETUOUS, WHEN YOU'RE ON YOUR WAY TO DOING WHAT'S RIGHT."

"OUR LIVES WHICH WERE ONCE PANORAMIC VISTAS AND ROLLING LANDSCAPES REACHING TO THE INFINITE HORIZON AND VANISHING POINT HAVE BEEN REDUCED TO A DIAGONAL FOUR-INCH IMAGE ON A CELL PHONE SCREEN."

"WHAT AMERICAN DOESN'T LOVE STARCH, GREASE AND SALT; THAT IS TO SAY, POTATO CHIPS; I.E., POOR MAN'S FRENCH-FRIES."

"For a real taste treat and a royal head-rush, <u>the only</u> fugu fish you'll ever what to eat, is the *Tora Fugu* McMuffin at the local McDonalds in Yamaguchi or Osaka Japan; because for extra credit during summer vacation, they teach the high school kids that work there how to properly gut and clean, prepare and deep fry um, and … they're a 'Finger licking good happy meal,' though you may not be able to feel your fingers or lips, or for that matter, move your tongue or swallow, and—they have the best super-sized *Frisson Fries* you'll ever eat, from 'lip tingling,' to … 'Someone call our Attorneys, the Police and Medical Examiner—and notify the next of kin' … '*In that freakin' order*!'"

"My blood pressure's always high when I'm
stressed-out and conscious,
but I'm not stressed when I'm unconscious …
<u>so take it then</u>, Doc!"

"It doesn't matter if you're forgotten
by humanity; as long as you're
remembered by Deity."

"Quite frankly and regrettably, the three
words that identified me during the
misspent part of my youth were:
<u>ingrate</u>, <u>punk</u> and <u>jackass</u>."

"If you love someone and don't get married,
not getting married won't change that,
nor will marrying them ensure it."

"It doesn't sweeten the deal if you rise and
shine bright and early at eight o'clock in
the morning, if you start work at 7:00 A.M.

"The formula is a simple one:
'Dress for success; stay naked and
you'll never make it.'"

"Trust me; I'm a writer and I've looked it up,
and 'ain't,' ain't a bona fide word."

"Keep your eye to the sky because:
'Red at morning sailors take warning;
red at night, sailors take delight;
mushroom clouds and gray, folks ...
it's Judgment Day.'"

"The world wraps sin up so beautifully;
it's sometimes hard to send it back
unopened."

"Integrity first: Everyone deserves your
A-game, unless your A-game is crap, in which
case, you've got to find a new game."

"If there's no hell there's no justice, and if
there's no justice it's not a moral universe,
and if it's not a moral universe there can be
no God, and if there is no God ...
there is no hope for man."

"September 11th and its aftermath to this
very day happened because there's evil in
the world ... and evil expresses itself,

AND WHEN IT EXPRESSES ITSELF, IT'S ANSWERED
WITH MORE EVIL."

"IN ALL HUMAN SOCIETIES FROM STONE AGE
PRIMITIVE TO THOSE HIGHLY-SOPHISTICATED AND
SECULARIZED, SIN HAS ALWAYS BEEN PERCEIVED
IN THE SPIRIT AND HEART OF MAN, AND THE
INESCAPABLE GNAWING GUILT OF SIN IN YOUR LIFE
MAKES YOU FEEL VULNERABLE—AND
VULNERABILITY MAKES YOU DEFENSIVE; THE NEED
TO BE DEFENSIVE MAKES YOU ANGRY, AND ANGER
MAKES YOU COMBATIVE—LEADING TO THE FAUX
ABSOLUTION AND JUSTIFICATION FOR WAR."

"BEAUTY CAN COVER UGLINESS AS LOVE CAN
COVER A MULTITUDE OF SINS."

"IF YOU MUST ERR, I'M SURE THE LORD WOULD
HAVE US ERR ON THE SIDE OF KINDNESS;
ERR ON THE SIDE OF GRACE; ERR ON THE SIDE OF
MERCY AND ERR ON THE SIDE OF LOVE."

"MOST PEOPLE NEVER GET THEIR BESTREWN
LIVES IN ORDER; THEY JUST ASSUME ALTERNATE
PATTERNS OF DISARRAY."

"BY THE LOOKS OF THINGS, I PERCEIVE THE
WORLD IN GENERAL, AND WE AMERICAS AND THE
WESTERN WORLD IN PARTICULAR, HAVE HUNG A
SIGN AROUND OUR NECKS THAT READS ...
'*DO NOT RESUSCITATE*.'"

"DON'T LET ANYONE BUT GOD INVITE YOU
TO YOUR OWN FUNERAL."

"I SHOULD'VE HAD THE SUSHI WITH THE SHIITES
AND THE SASHIMI WITH THE SUNNIS ...
TRY SAYING THAT THREE TIMES FAST!"

"WHO SAYS I CAN'T WRITE A COOKBOOK ENTITLED:
*HOW TO EAT LIKE A PIG AND GET AWAY WITH IT ...
AND YOU KNOW WHO YOU ARE*."

"WHAT IT LOOKS LIKE ISN'T ALWAYS WHAT IT IS,
AND LIKE MY OLD GRANDDADDY WHO WAS A
CRITICAL THINKER USED TO SAY— 'BOY, HOW'D
YOU KNOW IT WASN'T A FIVE-LEGGED DOG THAT
HAD TWO LEGS SHOT OFF?'"

"THE ONLY 'POSITIVE' ADDICTION IS ONE YOU'RE
NOT INVOLVED IN."

"IF AT FIRST YOU DON'T SUCCEED ...
FIND OUT WHY."

"LOOKS AREN'T ALL THAT IMPORTANT TO ME
HONEY ... I MEAN, *MY* LOOKS."

"THOUGH DEATH MAY DEFEAT US IN THIS LIFE,
IT CAN NEVER CONQUER US,
FOR GOD NEVER INTENDED DEATH TO BE THE END
OR ANSWER TO LIFE."

"THE GUYS I WORK WITH ARE EXTREMELY
FLEXIBLE AND GENERALLY MOVE AT FOUR
SPEEDS—CORAL, MOSS, GLACIAL AND ...
'I'M TAKEN' A HALF."

"SADDAM HUSSEIN? ... YES—AND CORRECT ME IF I'M WRONG, BUT WASN'T HE THAT BEWHISKERED, DEEP-FRIED NUT BALL SPIDER HOLE GUY IN TIGHTY-WHITIES WHOSE TWO SONS LOST A SHOOTOUT WITH THE UNITED STATES ARMY? I HEARD THAT AFTER A LIFETIME OF *WORKING IT*, HE MADE IT TO HIS FINAL DESTINATION AND REWARD AFTER A SHORT DANCE AT THE END OF A TIGHT ROPE."

"SO, YOU THINK YOU'VE GOT A LOT OF LIVING TO DO? ... WELL THEN, GO TO IT—
BUT JUST MAKE SURE THAT WHAT YOU CALL *LIVING*, ISN'T JUST SLOW MOTION DYING."

"IN THE LAND OF THE BLIND THE ONE-EYED MAN WINS THE ASS KICKING CONTEST—
AND THE ONE-LEGGED MAN IS USUALLY RUNNER-UP."

"IF BY RESTING COMFORTABLY YOU MEAN IN A VEGETATIVE COMA ... THEN YES—CHAIRMAN ARAFAT IS RESTING COMFORTABLY."
—THE "PALESTINIAN" AUTHORITY [NOV. "2004"]

"LIKE MY OLD GRANDDADDY USE TO SAY: 'BOY, YOU BEST GET YOUR STORY STRAIGHT, BECAUSE WHERE I COME FROM, YOU CAN'T MAKE KIELBASA OUT OF HOT SMOKE AND HOG-SHIT.'"

"MORE TO LIFE ISN'T SIMPLY MORE."

"IF YOU WANT TO AVOID A LOT OF STRESS IN LIFE, IGNORE THE CHATTER FROM THE CHEAP SEATS."

"I'M A CHRISTIAN, AND AS SUCH,
I KNOW THAT GOD AND HIS CHILDREN
ARE ALWAYS SAYING MORE THAN IS EVER
BEING HEARD IN THIS WORLD, BUT WHAT HIS
KIDS DO, <u>IS ALWAYS BEING NOTICED</u>."

"BETTER THAT ONE SHOULD DIE A THOUSAND
DEATHS, THAN SLAY SOMEONE WHO IS INNOCENT."

"ONE MUSTN'T AGITATE OR UPEND THE PRESENT,
FOR FEAR OF RESURRECTING THE PAST."

"THERE ARE TOO MANY OPTIONS IN LIFE THAT
ARE ALTERNATIVES TO DOING WHAT'S RIGHT—
AND EVEN WHAT'S RIGHT ...
HAS BECOME DEBATABLE."

"MANIFESTLY THE MOTTO OF THE MEDICAL
PROFESSION—<u>PRIMUM NON NOCERE</u>—
'FIRST DO NO HARM,'
NO LONGER APPLIES TO THE UNBORN."

"YOU CAN <u>ALWAYS</u> DO THE RIGHT THING,
IF YOU'RE PATIENT ENOUGH <u>NOT</u> TO DO THE
WRONG THING <u>FIRST</u>."

"AS A WRITER THE WORDS JUST COME TO ME,
AND ALL I HAVE TO DO IS WAIT,
AND, OF COURSE ... PUT THEM IN THE
RIGHT ORDER."

"LIKE MY OLD GRANDDADDY USE TO SAY— 'SON,
STAY AWAY FROM THEM STRIP-CLUBS, PORN-SITES,
NUDIE-BARS AND BEACHES, CUS THERE AIN'T NO
POINT IN SMELLIN' THE STEAK COOKIN',

IF YOU AIN'T INVITED TA THE "BARBECUE.'"

"JUST BECAUSE YOU'RE GOING DOWN DOESN'T MEAN YOU'RE THE FALL GUY."

"WITH INSTANT AND CONSTANT COMMUNICATION, THIS WORLD'S GOTTEN TO BE SO SMALL, THAT IF YOU SMILE, YOUR TEETH WILL HIT THE OZONE."

"AS HIS CHILDREN IN THE GARDEN, GOD WATCHED NASCENT HUMANITY STUMBLE AND FALL, AND THEN MADE A WAY FOR HIS LITTLE ONES, NOW INNOCENT AND FREE, TO RUN AND LAUGH AND PLAY AGAIN."

"I DO WHAT I DO BECAUSE I CAN, AND WHEN I CAN'T ... I WON'T."

"ALL WORDS HAVE MEANING TO HUMANITY, BUT ONLY GOD'S WORDS ARE IMPECCABLE AND HAVE POWER—AND IN THE BIBLE, GOD CHOSE TO SPEAK THROUGH LIGHTNING, OVER THE LIGHTNING-BUG."

"FRIENDS, LET'S JUST FACE IT, GET OVER IT AND GET ON WITH IT ... FAT, OUR FRIEND, IS FLAVOR— AND YOU NEED CHICKEN FAT TO MAKE <u>GOOD</u> CHICKEN SOUP AND EVERYTHING TASTES BETTER WITH BUTTER AND SALT IN IT—*AND GOOD ... IS GOOD!*"

"MY OLD GRANDDADDY ONCE TOLD ME WHEN I WAS YOUNG ... KID, STAY AWAY FROM THE 'WOMEN' WHO CAN WRITE THEIR NAME IN THE SNOW, AND GOT-AN 'APPLE' THAT BELONGS TO ADAM."

"I THINK IT WAS BENJAMIN FRANKLIN WHO SAID—
'I'D RATHER HAVE THEM TAP MY PHONE,
THAN TAP MY KEG.'"

"I'M FINDING THAT THE FUNK AND STANK WAFTING
OUT-A WASHINGTON THESE DAYS IS ENOUGH TO
KNOCK A BROKE-DICK DOG OF A GUT-WAGON."

"BROCCOLI, CABBAGE, CAULIFLOWER AND
BRUSSEL SPROUTS? ... NAH—THE ONLY VEGETABLE
WITH A HEAD I EVER EAT IS CHICKEN."

"IT TAKES A WHOLE LOT MORE TO BEING A MAN
THAN JUST SAYING SO."

"HAVE YOU EVER NOTICED THAT STEAK SIZZLING
ON A GRILL SOUNDS AN AWFUL LOT LIKE RAIN
FALLING ON A TIN ROOF, OR A COW PISSING ON A
FLAT ROCK?"

"DON'T TAKE ANY CRAP FROM THE UNIVERSE;
IF LIFE HANDS YOU LEMONS, GIVE IT A SWIFT KICK
IN THE BRAZIL NUTS."

"I THINK IT WAS EINSTEIN WHO SAID: E=M.C.
HAMMER ... '*NOT!*'"

"A 'PLAYER,' A.K.A. 'PLA-YA,' IS JUST A FOOL
THAT HASN'T BEEN CAUGHT YET."

"I RECKON IF YOU GET TO THE PLACE IN THE
ROAD WHERE YOU CAN'T COME BACK ...
YOU'VE GONE TOO FAR."

"Don't try to be something you're not,
unless it's a better human being."

"Don't kid yourself; there are no 'alternate
realities,' only alternatives <u>to</u> reality ...
which is fantasy."

"I'm easy to please and don't stand on
formality, so if all the chairs in the living
room are occupied, I'll just kick back, sit on
the floor and let my feet hang down."

"I can't speak for all, but as a Christian, I
don't want to face judgment and
punishment, nor have to administer it."

"God is understood and approached by faith
and is not limited by our human imagination."

"Often the most valuable though vilified
and hated tongues—are those that tell
the truth."

"The greatest freedom and privilege that
humanity has ever been afforded by Deity is
the right to choose—and the greatest
burden conferred—the need to obey."

"Always be careful when using a sharp
knife, because a knife doesn't care what or
whom it's cuttin'."

"In environments where imagination and creativity are deemed unnecessary, boredom, frustration and despondency will ensue."

"There's an inevitable price to pay for doing what's wrong—and often … what's right."

"Clinging to your past in the present keeps you from reaching your future."

"A prune is just a plum that spent too much time in the sun and now needs a facelift, and prosciutto's only ham that someone forgot to cook."

"Yah, I've lost a lot of hair—and tragically, all of it from my head."

"What is the North Korean word for an impacted and festering hemorrhoidal turd in the asshole of China?
—Answer: *Kim Jong-un*."

"The world is full of people who think life's problems can be solved with the stroke of a blade or the pull of a trigger."

"Jesus is the kind of God <u>we all need</u>; one who died for His friends <u>and</u> His enemies."

"WHY IS IT THAT THE IMAGE WE INSTANTLY CONJURE-UP WHEN WE THINK OF CAIN RISING UP AND SLAYING HIS BROTHER ABEL, IS ONE OF HIM USING A CLUB OR ROCK 'CAVEMAN STYLE' TO COMMIT THE NEFARIOUS DEED— THOUGH IT MAY NOT HAVE BEEN A BRUTAL ACT OF BASHING BARBARISM AT ALL, FROM WHICH THE VOICE OF ABEL'S SHED BLOOD CRIED OUT TO GOD FROM THE FIELD, BUT AN ELEGANTLY ADMINISTERED COLDBLOODED SLASH OR THRUST OF A RAZOR LIKE BLADE FROM THE MURDEROUS HAND OF HIS BROTHER CAIN." *(GENESIS 4:8-:10)*

"I DON'T WEAR MUSCLE SHIRTS THAT SHOWCASE MY MUSCLES; I'VE GOT MUSCLES THAT MAKE FOR EYE-POPPING SHIRTS."

"IF YOU CAN LAUGH WHEN YOU'RE ALONE; YOU'RE GOING TO BE ALL RIGHT."

"IN A COSMOS RULED BY DIVINITY, THE 'INEVITABILITY' OF HUMAN MORTALITY IS NOT INEVITABLE."

"ALL YOU HAVE TO DO FOR SOME PEOPLE IS GIVE THEM ROOM AND A CHANCE TO ESCAPE THEIR LOT IN LIFE, AND THEY'LL RUN WITH IT TOWARD SUCCESS, THOUGH MODERN AMERICA IS NOW REPLETE WITH THOSE WHO'D RATHER BE SELF-MEDICATED, THAN -MOTIVATED, OR -EDUCATED."

"WE CHRISTIANS IN THE WESTERN WORLD OF THE TWENTY-FIRST CENTURY OFTEN THINK THAT WE'RE ENTITLED TO LIVE-OUT ALL OF OUR DAYS IN ABUNDANCE, PLACIDITY AND PEACE,

WHEN MOST OF THE CITED BELIEVERS IN THE
BIBLE LIVED OUT <u>THEIR LIVES</u> IN DEARTH,
PAIN AND EXQUISITE DRAMA."

"IT'S LIKE THE BLIND LEADING THE STUPID,
BECAUSE IF HARDCORE HIP-HOP RAPPERS
STARTED WEARING FUZZY PURPLE TOILET SEAT
COVERS AS BERETS, I'M QUITE CERTAIN THE
MERCHANTS WOULDN'T BE ABLE TO KEEP THEM
ON THE SHELVES FROM NEW YORK CITY TO
TOKYO JAPAN."

"IF THEY STICK IT OUT WITH YOU WHEN YOU'RE A
NOBODY; IT'D ONLY BE REASONABLE TO ASSUME
THAT YOU'D STICK IT OUT WITH THEM WHEN
YOU'RE A SOMEBODY."

"WAKE ME WHEN IT'S OVER—
BUT ONLY IF WE WIN."

"JUDGING BASED ON THE CONTENT OF THE
CHARACTER RATHER THAN THE COLOR OF THE
SKIN IS NOT AFFORDED COLLECTIVELY, BUT
INDIVIDUALLY."

"BIRDS OF PRAY ARE HERE TO STAY;
ON THE JOB TILL JUDGMENT DAY."

"I'LL CONSIDER A MAN A FRIEND, BUT ONLY IF HE
DOESN'T CONSIDER ME A FOOL FOR DOING SO."

"DON'T LOOK DOWN UPON THE POOR,
BECAUSE IT'S NOT A SIN TO BE POOR,
BUT IT'S A DISGRACE TO BE BASE."

"The battlefield is earth;
we of humanity are gladiators,
and the last enemy to be defeated is death."

"With high technology surveillance and face recognition software, cell phones, swipe cards and monitored 21st century public and private media, you can rest assured that all of us are now safely hidden in plain view of the eye in the sky."

"Truth and facts are two of those pesky things you can't be 'relatively positive' about."

"No one goes back in history far enough to prove the truth of their advisory's point; only far enough back to justify their own."

"What's the point of being nuts if you're not good at it?"

"If nothing in this life ever brings tears to your eyes—pray for God to change that."

"Though it breaks your heart, better to weep at the painful truth reviled, then laugh and rejoice in oblivious ignorance."

"As a Christian, how good would my life have to become here for me not to want to leave?"

"When I was young in another time, the kid's I knew were unapologetic for having distinct identities and unique, creative, individual personalities; today, they're just morphing and being absorbed into the mind-numbing homogeny of each other."

"When what was once considered bizarre becomes the no longer noticed mainstream, then that which was mainstream will stand-out and morph into the new bizarre, and therefore, be on the cusp of cutting edge chic."

"An <u>immortal</u> Untouchable could never appreciate or identify with a <u>mortal</u> Gladiator."

"Death is not a mystery to the dead, but a mystery revealed."

"Better to forget a man's a criminal and treat him accordingly, than forget that he's human and treat him as such."

"Marie Antoinette would never get me to eat cake, not even on my birthday, because I much prefer my sister's homemade apple pie."

"All we mortals are Gladiators, and the last enemy to be defeated ... is Death."

"This present world is a very evil place with smatterings of good and flashes of Glory."

"God's the only one who can make a man
greater than he's willing to be."

"I've always found politicians to be mere
shape-shifters with alacrity."

"For those who <u>won't</u> listen, it <u>doesn't</u>
matter if they <u>can't</u> hear."

"You know you're in a country with great
dental care, if you're seventy years old
and you can still crack Brazil nuts with
your front teeth."

"The spirit and heart of man is such, that if
it were to gain the whole world and ten
thousand years in which to enjoy its
<u>earthly pleasures</u>, it would never be
enough for a being that was so elegantly
made and meant for an <u>eternity of glory</u>."

"In a democracy those who lead are
responsible for their leadership,
and those who follow are responsible
for the same."

"'But we were just following orders!' ...
'Really?' ... I mean, 'Freakin' really!' ...
and the consequences thereof as well?"

"Anyone can be great in the Kingdom of God
because the approval of men is not a
prerequisite."

"In the Garden, nascent humanity barely
had a chance to live, before we started
to die."

"We're living in a brave new world
populated with puppets
dancing on the same taut cords."

"The whole world is full of mimics, and if
you're going to be a mimic, don't mimic the
mimics, mimic an original."

"Don't be offended if someone claims
you're up to something, because everyone's
up to something."

"We're all just raggedy men navigating
in a raggedy-ass world."

"Life is a minefield; expect delays."

"I do love the humble potato, even if it's
sliced razor thin, salted,
boiled in oil and stuffed into a large
polypropylene bag."

"I know what I know; everything else is
just guesswork."

"My shrink told me I'm not crazy,
but it's only a temporary condition."

"Too quick to kill; too numb to merciful
reason has forever been the hallmark
of humanity."

"Death is at once the great equalizer and
the great divider."

"'Vengeance is the Lord's' to be sure,
but temporal retribution He has
bequeathed to mankind."

"There's a secular world, and a religious
world—and then there's Christianity."

"I'm a patriot of what America once was;
a proud patriot of what's left of America."

"Like my old granddad used to say:
'If you really want-um gone; just give-um a
warm beer and tell-um to beat-it.'"

"God's assessment of humanity has always
been that the heart of man is the domicile
of a madman."

"In America there's always some
phenomenon sweeping the nation, and I'm
dearly waiting for the phenomenon of love
reason, peace and quietness to kick in."

"The injustices in our lives are justified
because of our injustice."

"PEACE IS THE PREROGATIVE OF THE SPIRIT,
HEART AND MIND AND IS NOT DETERMINED BY
ONE'S CIRCUMSTANCE OR ENVIRONMENT."

"IF PUSH COMES TO SHOVE IT'S GOING TO END
VERY BADLY FOR SOMEBODY
AND IT'S NOT GOING TO BE ME."

"PRAYING FOR THE DEAD ONLY SERVES
THE LIVING."

"I SWATTED AT A BEE OR A FLY OR A FLEA LET IT
BE LET IT BE WOE IS ME WOE IS ME NOW I FLEE
AND I FLY TO THE SEA CAN'T YOU SEE MON AMI?"

"THINKING OUTSIDE OF 'THE BOX' IS A GREAT TOOL
TO EMPLOY, AS LONG AS YOU DON'T WAIT UNTIL
YOU'RE IN YOUR CASKET."

"LIFE IS FULL OF RANDOM AND SEEMINGLY
INNOCUOUS 'LOOSE THREADS' ALL OF WE HUMANS
HAVE FOREVER BEEN INCLINED TO BE
ABSENTMINDEDLY PULLING AND PICKING-AT OVER
<u>HERE</u>, WHICH WILL INEVITABLY MAKE A 'BUTTON'
FALL OFF THAT'S HOLDING CRUCIAL THINGS
TOGETHER <u>OVER THERE</u>."

"EMBRACING DIVERSITY IN HUMANITY IS A GOOD
THING, HOWEVER, ONE MUST REALIZE AND
CONSIDER THAT THE ULTIMATE RESULT OF
PURSUING IT WITHOUT LIMITS AND GIVEN ENOUGH
TIME, WILL INEVITABLY LEAD TO HOMOGENY AND
THEREFORE THE END OF DIVERSITY."

"AMERICA THE ONCE INTREPID AND EXPANSIVE,
IS NOW ALLOWING HERSELF TO BE COLONIZED
AND CANNIBALIZED BY THE REST OF *THE HUNGRY*
WORLD."

"THE SAD TRUTH IS THAT VIOLENCE WORKS, BUT
ONLY IF YOU'RE MORTAL; JUST ASK ANY
TERRORIST."

[SATAN'S EPITAPH]
"HE HAD HIS DAY IN THE SUN, FADED TO BLACK …
AND HE'S DONE."

"EVEN THOUGH IT'S REALLY EASY TO DO,
DON'T LEARN HOW TO BE OLD, STAY YOUNG."
"I DON'T WANT TO MERELY SUCCEED IN LIFE;
I WANT TO SUCCEED AT LIFE."

"'HOW CLEAN ARE COCKROACHES,' YOU ASK …
I DON'T KNOW, HOW CLEAN DO YOU NEED
THEM TO BE?"

"IN MY NEIGHBORHOOD WHEN I WAS YOUNG,
YOU DIDN'T HAVE TO BE A THUG OR TOUGH-GUY TO
LIVE THERE, YOU JUST HAD TO WANT TO."

"WE'RE LIVING IN A VERY REAL WORLD, WITH VERY
UNREALISTIC PEOPLE, LIVING VERY REAL
FANTASIES AND SUFFERING VERY REAL
CONSEQUENCES."

"IF YOU'RE AN <u>OBEDIENT</u> CHRISTIAN,
YOU <u>CAN'T</u> BE A <u>HOSTILE WITNESS</u> THAT
<u>REFUSES TO TESTIFY</u>."

"IN THIS PRESENT AGE PEACE CAN'T BE BROUGHT
TO ALL SITUATIONS, FOR MORE AND MORE OFTEN,
THINGS ARE NOT IN NEED OF THE PEACE WE SEEK,
BUT A RECKONING WE DESERVE."

"WE OF MODERN HUMANITY ARE A SPIDER
CAUGHT IN ITS OWN ANCIENT AND
GLISTENING WEB."

"YOU'LL KNOW THAT YOU'RE MATURING IN THE
PRESENCE OF GREATNESS, WHEN YOUR HEAD
STARTS TO FIT YOUR HAT."

"SOME PEOPLE ARE OLD AND ANGRY SIMPLY
BECAUSE THEY'RE ANGRY ABOUT BEING OLD."

"WE'RE ON THE CUSP OF A FUTURE WHEREIN
NO AMOUNT OF THINKING WILL ANSWER THE
QUESTIONS."

"IT'S AMAZING WHAT'S DOABLE IF YOU'RE
WILLING TO DO IT."

"LIFE IS VERY EXPERT AT KILLING THE LIVING."

"I SUSPECT THE PRICE OF HIGH-PRICED CALL GIRLS
IS SO HIGH THESE DAYS, BECAUSE THE STANDARDS
OF PHILANDERING MEN ARE SO LOW."

"OH, IT'S JUST A '_ME_' THING ...
BECAUSE I DON'T REVEAL _MY_ SOURCES,
_MY_ METHODS OR _MY_ MADNESS."

"Not asking the wrong questions doesn't
insure the right answers."

"I find I have great organizational skills, as
long as I'm not compelled to manage a
steaming hot pile of chaos; which
incidentally and if I'm not mistaken,
is my current job description."

"We're living in times in which <u>only the
accountable</u> are held to account
and made to answer for their justification."

"Knives are cutting tools that consist of
two parts, essentially a blade and a
handle; nowadays however, the high-end
high-tech knives are so complicated, you
need an instruction manual and a set of
tools to keep them from falling apart."

"Just remember, if God has a great purpose
for your life, you can't be dead
to fulfill it."

"The greatest problem that modern
humanity is facing is that the 'weeds,'
are relentlessly encroaching upon
and aggressively choking-out
that which is producing the fruit."

"To succeed in this life,
somebody in the know has to notice you."

"By design, the internet and social media are dumbing-down everyone that uses them —if it isn't already a *fait accompli*."

"Most of humanity is living in an imaginary dream world with no one so inclined as to wake them up."

"In this life too much of our time is being spent getting everyone's head back to what passes for normal"

"You can't become like your enemy in hopes of defeating him, or you'll defeat yourself for him."

"Human life on planet earth has proven to be a natural state, oscillating between the twilight of frantic terror and languid melancholy."

"If I've asked Jesus to get involved in my lot, don't dare tell me not to get my hopes up.

"I have dreams too, but not about those who dream about me."

"Don't be ashamed about being ashamed if you have reason to be ashamed, for it is nowadays, a rare quality to possess."

"I'M NO MEMBER OF THE N.R.A.—AND YES I'M ARMED—AND I'M NO THREAT TO YOU WHATSOEVER—UNLESS YOU TRY TO DISARM ME."

"YOU KNOW I NEVER THOUGHT I HAD THAT MUCH TO SAY, UNTIL I STARTED WRITING."

"BETTER TO <u>ELIMINATE</u> THE PROBLEM THAN ATTEMPT TO <u>MITIGATE</u> THE CONSEQUENCES THEREOF."

[TONGUE TWISTER]
SAY (3) TIMES FAST
"WE MAY HAVE MET ONCE BEFORE."

"YOU'RE NOT A DEFEATIST OR A LOSER IF YOU BELIEVE YOU'RE NEVER GOING TO WIN IN THIS LIFE, BUT YOU ARE IF YOU BELIEVE GOD'S NOT."

"I'D NEVER MAKE-IT AS A SECOND LIEUTENANT WITH A ROADMAP AND A COMPASS, BECAUSE THE ONLY PERCEIVABLE SENSE OF DIRECTION I POSSESS IS—UP AND DOWN, FORWARD AND BACKWARDS AND SIDE TO SIDE."

"HERE EVERYONE LOOKS INSANE, BECAUSE THE INSANE LOOK AT THE SANE AS THOUGH THEY WERE INSANE, AND THE SANE LOOK AT THE INSANE THE SAME."

"WHO BUT GOD KNOWS? —AND OH BUT GOD KNOWS!—IF ONE OF THESE LITTLE ONES, THAT COULD HAVE BEEN BORN, SHOULD HAVE BEEN BORN, WOULD HAVE BEEN BORN … WHO THEY

COULD HAVE BEEN, WOULD THEY HAVE BEEN, SHOULD THEY HAVE BEEN."

"THE <u>PERMANENT</u> UNDERCLASS IS PERMANENTLY SO, BECAUSE THEY'RE PLEASED TO NO LONGER HAVE TO REACH, AND LOATHE TO LATCH-ON-TO AND NOT LET GO."

"DON'T EVER PRAY THAT THE WICKED CEASE TROUBLING YOU, FOR THEY SHOULD TROUBLE YOU—RATHER, PRAY THAT THEY CEASE BEING WICKED, FOR IF YOU MERELY CEASE BEING TROUBLED BY THEIR EVIL THEN THEY WIN AND EVERYONE LOSES."

"PAY HEED IF YOU NEED, AND CULTIVATE A PASSION TO SUCCEED WITHOUT GREED— AND YOU SHALL INDEED MY PRECIOUS SEED."

"EARTH HAS PROVEN ITSELF TO BE A PLANET THAT NEEDS TO HAVE A SIGH HUNG AROUND HER NECK THAT READS: *<u>HERE THERE BE MONSTERS</u>*."

"I'VE COME TO REALIZE THAT IT'S OFTEN THE LITTLEST PIECE OF SHIT THAT CAUSES THE BIGGEST STINKING PROBLEMS."

"WHEN BREWERIES AND DISTILLERIES 'LIQUEFY THEIR ASSETS' IT'S A VERY GOOD THING; WHEN THE REST OF US ARE COMPELLED TO DO SO FOR FIGHT, FLIGHT OF FRIGHT ... PERHAPS NOT SO MUCH."

"We're innocent of all but being human;
which makes us guilty."

"Embracing the diversity in others carte
blanche will not remedy or mitigate their
dysfunction, nor ameliorate the perceived
guilt of those attempting the amelioration."

"One mustn't merely embrace the diversity
of the other, but their humanity which is
our commonality."

"In the 'Garden of deviation,' it seems that
diversity was the consequence of sin and
the further catalyst for it, even unto this
very day."

"We all of us have allowed cell phones and
social media to turn us into
vapid drones and distracted dunces."

"Too many have no story to tell for they've
written it in the wind; the dust of the road
and on the sand of the seashore."

"Remember that the only thing
that can't be taken from you is that
which you don't possess."

"If you must be negative, be negative
about things that are negative
not those that are positive."

"IF AT FIRST YOU DON'T SUCCEED—
GET SOMEONE ELSE TO DO IT RIGHT."

"I'VE BEEN NOTICING THE MODERN PHENOMENON
THAT RED TRAFFIC LIGHTS AT INTERSECTIONS NO
LONGER SEEM TO DETER PEDESTRIANS FROM
CROSSING AGAINST TRAFFIC—AND STOP SIGNS
HAVE BEEN REDUCED TO MERE SUGGESTIONS
WITH THE UBIQUITOUS 'ROLLING STOP OPTION.'"

"YOU DON'T HAVE TO BE GREAT IN THE KINGDOM
OF MEN TO BE GREAT IN THE KINGDOM OF GOD."

"IF YOU DON'T LIKE THE ANSWER,
WHY KEEP ASKING THE QUESTION?"

"SKUNKS HAVE BEEN AROUND FOR A LONG TIME;
ALMOST AS LONG AS POLITICIANS,
BUT MUCH UNLIKE POLITICIANS, THEY *CAN ONLY*
SPRAY IN ONE DIRECTION AT A TIME."

"EVERY LITTLE CHOICE WE MAKE AGAINST
THE TRUTH MAKES TYRANNY AND
BONDAGE POSSIBLE."

"IT'S HARD TO HAVE TO JUDGE STARVING MEN."

"ONCE THE ENEMY HAS DECEIVED YOU INTO
DISTRACTION, HE'LL DEVOUR YOU WITH
DESTRUCTION."

"WHEN THE FONT IS TOO SMALL IT LOSES IMPACT;
WHEN IT'S TOO LARGE IT LOSES YOUR EMBRACE."

"It's hard to stop folks from pursuing what's evil if it's not against the law."

"Those who've never suffered want and feel no need to be thankful are the most helpless and pathetic of us all."

"There yet exists the hopeful myth that what one sews, one shall not also reap."

"Sometimes one must forgo peace to establish one's righteousness, for the prerogative of righteousness is the foundation upon which peace rests and to which it is beholden."

"Too many are building a bridge to nowhere fast."

"Most of humanity is so helpless, in not having someone to give thanks to."

"Only those who know God fear Him, and *only* those that *don't* fear Him will ultimately face Him in judgment and be catapulted from 'no fear'—to 'know' fear, from 'No God' to ... 'Oh God!' and finally from, 'Don't cast me away!' to—'Oh Lord! I want to stay!' but hay! ... It's now Judgment Day."

"Yes—Human Resources made it quite explicitly clear to me that the most important prerequisite qualification for

MY CURRENT JOB IS THE ABILITY TO LOWER MY HEAD AND SHAKE IT SLOWLY FROM SIDE TO SIDE AS I SHUFFLE, WHILE REPEATEDLY MUTTERING THE PHRASE '*UN-BE-FREAKIN'-LIEVABLE.*'"

"ONE OF MY FAVORITE PASTORS ONCE SHARED WITH US THIS OBSERVATION FROM HIS PULPIT ... 'MAN, I'M PREACHING SO GOOD, I THINK I SHOULD START TAKING NOTES ON MYSELF.'"

"PEOPLE RARELY RECOGNIZE THE BEGINNING OF THE END WHEN IT COMES, BUT NONE OF US WILL MISS THE SIGNIFICANCE OF THE END ITSELF."

"LIFE IS SUCH, THAT THE DEEPER YOU SEND YOUR ROOTS, THE MORE PAINFUL THE EXTRACTION, FOR WE LIGHT FOOTED PILGRIMS JUST PASSING THROUGH AREN'T MEANT TO BE HERE FOREVER."

"YAH I KNOW GINGER AND THERMITE, AND THEY SOUND TO ME LIKE A HOT COUPLE, BUT A MATCH MADE JUST A LITTLE LOWER THAN HEAVEN."

"IN A WORLD FULL OF PEOPLE WHO HAVE CHOSEN TO FILTER-OUT THEIR TACTILE HUMANITY THROUGH CELLULAR DEVICES; I STILL PREFER <u>FACE TO FACE</u> AND <u>MOUTH TO EAR</u> COMMUNICATION, AND WHEN I ASK A FRIEND TO 'FACE ME,' I FULLY EXPECT FOR THEM TO ACTUALLY BE THERE, WATCH THEM TURN AROUND AND TAKE A STEP CLOSER, LET ME SEE THEIR EYES, AND ACTUALLY ... 'FACE <u>ME</u>!'"

"DON'T TELL ME WHAT I SHOULD'VE BEEN; TELL ME WHAT I CAN BE."

"DENIAL AND HOLLYWOOD'S FANCY AND TENDER NOTIONS ASIDE, MODERN HUMANITY HAS ALWAYS BEEN PRECARIOUSLY ARTICULATED ON THE CUSP OF <u>INEXTRICABLE</u> SELF-IMPOSED OBLIVION."

"<u>YES,</u> PRAISE JESUS ... BUT '<u>OH</u>' WHAT A WORLD!"

"MAYBE IN OUR LIVES IT'S NOT WHAT HAPPENED BUT WHAT DIDN'T HAPPEN THAT MAKES ALL THE DIFFERENCE IN THE WORLD ... FOR BETTER OR FOR WORSE."

"MOST PEOPLE DON'T PUT THEIR LIVES ON THE LINE; THEY'RE PUT THERE BY OTHERS."

"THIS WORLD WAS ONCE A RICH YOKE; NOW A HALLOWED-OUT SHELL."

"IF IT WASN'T FOR THE MARVEL OF T.P., EVERY TIME I'D SHAVE WITH A BRAND-NEW DOUBLE-EDGED RAZORBLADE, IT WOULD BE DEATH BY A THOUSAND CUTS."

"MY POLICY IS THAT IT'S NOT MY BUSINESS, BUT IT'LL BE MY BUSINESS, IF THEY MAKE IT MY BUSINESS."

"IT IS A VERY TROUBLED AND TROUBLING WORLD, AND THOSE THAT AREN'T TROUBLED BY IT, ARE THE MOST GRAVELY TROUBLED OF US ALL."

"A LOSER THAT CHOOSES <u>NOT</u> TO HANG WITH OTHER LOSERS, EVEN IF HE MUST STAND ALONE, IS WELL ON HIS WAY TO BEING A VICTOR."

"OH-YAH, I KNOW THE SONG *MY GUY*, BY MARY WELLS; MOTOWN 1964, RIGHT?
GREAT SONG, GREAT LYRICS! —AND I KNOW YOU LIKE SINGING AND WHISTLING IN THE SHOWER AND THAT YOU'RE RATHER NEW AT THIS THING ... BUT DUDE! ... YOU'RE IN A MAXIMUM-SECURITY FEDERAL PRISON! ... I'M JUST SAYIN'."

"FROM HIS VANTAGE POINT, GOD CAN SEE THE WHOLE BATTLEFIELD—AND HE KNOWS THAT HUMANITY IS NOT GOING TO WIN THIS ONE."

"HEALING AND FREEDOM ALWAYS COME, WHEN THE '<u>WHO</u>' WE'RE SUPPOSED TO BE, EXPOSES THE '<u>WHO</u>' WE'RE PRETENDING TO BE."

"FOR TOO MANY THE EPIPHANY COMES AFTER THE VERDICT IS READ, AND FOR FAR TOO MANY MORE ... NOT EVEN THEN."

"BEING RETIRED IS THE ONLY ELEMENT OF MY JOB THAT I LOVE, WHICH IS WHY ...
'YOU CAN'T TOUCH THIS!' ...
'YOU CAN'T TOUCH THIS!'

"I BELIEVE THAT *SENSITIVE GRAFFITI REMOVER SPRAYS* ARE NO DOUBT DESIGNED FOR THE NAMBY-PAMBIES WHO MIGHT BE IN NEED OF GETTING UNWANTED GRAFFITI OFF THEIR SENSITIVE ASSES, BITS AND PIECES."

"GOOD NEWS TRAVELS FAST, OFTEN WITH BAD NEWS SNAPPING AT ITS HEELS."

"It's a tender notion, but I have no illusions or delusions; if we haven't done it by now, humanity is not going to save ourselves."

"Sometimes you don't remember what you're missing till you come back home."

"I'm not worried about what sticks to my feet at work, or from the other side of the tracks, or the marketplace; I'm more concerned about what cleaves to my very own soul everlasting."

"You can't make peace with <u>death</u> any more than you can with the devil, for it is the last enemy that <u>must</u> be defeated."

"Have you ever wondered who <u>the first</u> guy was that ever burned the roof of his mouth eating food that was too hot, too fast? *...What a loser!*"

"The world isn't changing, it's just continuing with a fresh batch of players, victims and witnesses."

"Healing when it comes always starts nebulous at the corners and edges of our lives granulating its way from the peripheries, into perfection and plain view; our scars and the fading memories of our pain notwithstanding."

"SOMETIMES THE ONLY SENSE YOU CAN MAKE OF
IT ALL IS THAT IT'S NONSENSE."

"WITH GOD YOU NEVER KNOW, FOR IT MIGHT ALL
JUST END WITH A BIGGER 'BANG' THAN IT ALL
STARTED WITH."

"A PATRIOT <u>OF ONLY</u> WHAT AMERICA <u>ONCE WAS</u>,
IS A PATRIOT NO MORE."

"FORETHOUGHT OF MALICE AGAINST THAT WHICH
IS EVIL AND WICKED IS A RIGHTEOUS ACT,
AS SURELY AS MALICE OF FORETHOUGHT AGAINST
THOSE WHO ARE INNOCENT IS AN ACT OF EVIL."

"I DON'T KNOW WHAT I'M MISSING, UNLESS IT'S ON
THE WAY.

"ONE DAY THERE'LL BE PEACE AND JUSTICE, BUT
IN THIS LIFE ONLY THE FLEETING AND MITIGATING
AMELIORATION OF ANGUISH."

"IT'S NOT ALWAYS THE MAN WITH THE GUN IN HIS
HAND THAT DOESN'T END-UP NOT DEAD."

"WHEN YOU FIND YOURSELF UNDER ATTACK IT'S
USUALLY BECAUSE YOU'RE EITHER
DOING WHAT'S WRONG OR DOING WHAT'S RIGHT."

"STORY OF MY LIFE; NOW MY VISION'S GREAT,
BUT I GOT NO VIEW!"

"WITH NO CONTROL OVER OUR BORDERS,
AMERICA IS NO LONGER A MELTING POT,
BUT AN OVER-SPICED AND UNDER-COOKED,
SEETHING SWIRLING POT OF *CRAZY STEW AND
GLOBAL GUMBO*, AND A VERITABLE FREAK-SHOW
IN A BOWL."

"DON'T GET IN THE HABIT OF ANSWERING
QUESTIONS NOBODY'S ASKING."

"THE TWEAKING OF THE CREATIVE PROCESS OF
THE ADVERTISERS ADDS CAMPAIGN FOR THE
NATIONAL CATTLEMEN'S BEEF ASSOCIATION,
EVENTUALLY CLEAR ON THE CONCEPT:
(1.) BEEF, IT'S WHAT'S CLOGGING YOUR ARTERIES.
(2.) BEEF, IT'LL BLOW YOUR HEART OUT.
(3.) BEEF, IT AIN'T YOUR GRANDSON'S TOFU.
(4.) BEEF, IT HAD PARENTS.
(5.) BEEF? "HELLS YAH!"
(6.) BEEF, IT'S WHAT'S FOR DINNER. ✔ ✔ ✔ ✔

"THOSE WHO DON'T EXPECT MUCH OUT OF LIFE
ARE SURE TO BE SATISFIED."

"THE RIGHTEOUS EXPECT GOOD IN THE END;
THE WICKED ONLY HOPE OF ESCAPE."

"WAGING WAR IS HORROR; FIGHTING CRIME IS
HORROR; THE CONSEQUENCE OF SIN IS HORROR."

"MAN'S REACH HAS ALWAYS EXCEEDED
HIS GRASP, BUT GOD'S REACH HAS ALWAYS
REACHED MAN."

"Much of what you cite is what I do;
what I've done; not what and who I am."

"I understand it can all be taken away;
I can be taken away from it;
it can all be taken away from me;
it can all be taken away from all of us."

"Sometimes the Lord allows distasteful
things on our watch because
He knows we can be trusted with them."

"'Gee! are they fireworks or are they
gunshots?' ... well, here where I live,
sometimes both; the fireworks to mask
the gunshots."

"The least I can do in this life is not hinder
anyone else's progress—
and the most I can do ... I have no idea."

"God is the Author of Life;
humanity paradoxically the mortal
architects of death."

"The silent scream is merely one
that is not heard."

"It is an angry world replete with people
who no longer cultivate peace in their
lives; they succumb and amass fury."

"It's what I do, what I've done, not who I am."

"As Christians, if we don't do it,
nobody else will."

"Sometimes peace comes only on the heels
of a river of tears."

"The ultimate power of control is over ones
very own spirit."

"Creativity is a process not an event,
therefore: Don't try and hustle to get it all
down and done in one sitting, for you may
just find-out, that your true creativity
kicked-in soon after you've submitted your
final draft."

"Sometimes the scenario is reminiscent of
pursuing a seemingly arrogant and
manifestly well fed fruit fly that keeps
returning to your stash of fresh fruit, and
despite your best efforts at trying to smash
him between the palms of your hands and
failing repeatedly, you relent, for you come
to the epiphany that the appetite of one
exceedingly deft and elusive fruit fly, is
not worth your effort expended and
creativity exhausted in ultimately ending
his petty theft and reign of emotional
terror over you."

"Fake news, fake media, fake reality …
Ain't life grand?"

"DON'T FRET ABOUT IT; SOMETIMES EVEN IN THE
HANDS OF A MASTER, THE WOOD LEADS THE
BLADE WHERE IT WANTS IT TO GO."

"I LOVE TAKING POWERNAPS; THEY'RE THE BEST
SPENT THREE HOURS OF MY WORKDAY."

"A SLOB DOES NOT RECOGNIZE DISORDER AND
HAVOC WHEN HE WREAKS IT,
NOR APPRECIATES ORDER WHEN HE INHABITS IT."

"DON'T GET IN THE BAD HABIT OF TELLING FOLKS
WHAT THEY WANT TO HEAR;
TELL THEM WHAT THEY NEED TO KNOW."

"I HAVE A LOT OF BRANDS IN THE FIRE OF MY MIND
AND NOT ALL OF THEM MINE."

"IF GOD WANTS ALL OF HUMANITY TO BE <u>SAVED</u>;
THE PRICE FOR IT HAS ALREADY BEEN <u>PAID</u> AND
ALL OF US HAVE <u>FREE</u> WILL, THEN ONLY <u>WE</u>, CAN
NEGATE THAT."

"TOO MANY PRODUCE AND REPRODUCE,
BUT NOTHING OF QUALITY."

"OH, YOU CAN BELIEVE THAT LIFE IS ORDERED AND
ORCHESTRATED, JUST NOT BY US."

"EVENTUALLY EVERYONE WHO'S DOING EVIL
PULLS A PIN ON THE WRONG GRENADE."

"NO MATTER HOW CLEVER OR FLEET IN OUR
ESCAPE, THE TRUTH IS ALWAYS JUST THAT
MUCH FASTER AND WAITING FOR US THERE
WHEN WE ARRIVE."

"I DON'T SEE ANY REASON IN HAVING TO TAKE
A SHOWER TOMORROW MORNING
IF I DIDN'T GET DIRTY TODAY."

"YOU KNOW YOU'VE GOT OCD WHEN THEY
COMPEL YOU TO DIG YOUR OWN GRAVE, AND YOU
MAKE QUITE CERTAIN THERE'S AN EQUAL AMOUNT
OF DIRT ON BOTH SIDES OF THE HOLE BEFORE
YOU'RE DONE."

"WITH A NATIONAL DEBT OF 19 <u>TRILLION</u> DOLLARS
AT THIS WRITING THAT OUR LENDERS WILL NEVER
LIVE TO SEE US PAY BACK, AND AMERICA
PRODUCING NOTHING OF SIGNIFICANT VALUE ANY
MORE, WE ARE HOWEVER, YET A CHIC BRAND THAT
THE WORLD KEEPS BUYING INTO—AND FOR
REASONS KNOWN ONLY TO THEM."

"HOW MANY POSSIBLE *COMBINATIONS* CAN THERE
BE TO DOING WHAT'S RIGHT?
... ONLY ONE, WHICH MAKES IT A *PERMUTATION.*"

"IT'S NOT STARDUST BUT SAWDUST THAT MOST
DREAMS ARE MADE OF."

"I ALWAYS USE PREMIUM CORNED BEEF WHEN I
MAKE CORNED BEEF SANDWICHES, BECAUSE IT
GIVES ME A MUCH MORE PRONOUNCED CORNED
BEEF FLAVOR THAN WHEN I USE BOLOGNA."

"YAH I LOVE CORNED BEEF; WHICH IS NOT TO BE
CONFUSED WITH 'CORNERED' BEEF,
WHICH IS JUST THE BULL THAT DIDN'T GET AWAY."

"THOSE WHO TOUT THE CATCHPHRASE
'REPRODUCTIVE RIGHTS' AND PROTEST AND OPINE
THAT NO ONE KNOWS WHEN LIFE BEGINS, WILL
ONE DAY FIND OUT WHEN LIFE FOR THEM ENDS."

"GREAT TACTICAL GEAR AND TRAINING DOESN'T
MAKE A MAN A HERO—BUT BEING IN THE RIGHT
PLACE AT THE RIGHT TIME DOING THE RIGHT THING
FOR THE RIGHT MOTIVES DOES."

"YAH, I'VE GOT A LOT OF FIBER IN MY DIET;
AFTER BRUSHING MY TEETH,
I HAVE TO FLOSS MY TOOTHBRUSH."

"DON'T WORRY ABOUT GETTING RID
OF THE 'FLY-SHIT' IN YOUR LIFE;
HOW'S ABOUT GETTIN' RID OF THE DAMN 'FLIES!'"

"I DON'T HAVE ALL THE ANSWERS, BUT THE
TERRORISTS SEEM TO THINK THEY HAVE ALL THE
ANSWERS ... DEATH!"

"A POLITICIAN SAYING 'NO THANKS' TO MONEY
OFFERED, IS LIKE A SNOT-SLINGING BOOZER
SAYING 'NO' TO THE NEXT DRINK ON THE HOUSE."

"SOMETIMES STUFF AROUND HERE HAPPENS THAT
MAKES ME THINK I'M IN AN EPISODE
OF THE THREE STOOGES, EXCEPT AT THE TIME,
I'M THE ONLY STOOGE IN THE HOUSE."

"In this modern antithetical age of hyper instant and continuous global cellular 'commutation,' we're paradoxically growing infinitely more efficient at avoiding any kind of genuine and intimate human contact."

"I hope to live in a day to come when I will never long for the past."

"My buddy said to me: 'Hay Bro., I'm up to 340 Lbs.; I said, 340 Lbs. of what; he said: 'Dude, you don't wanna know.'"

"Even though it's a distasteful task, if you're compelled to do it anyways, you might as well do it splendidly."

"I see the world moving too fast in every wrong direction—and we're almost there."

"It's not the past that haunts me but the future."

"Fear and fatigue are no-good reasons for quitting, or pain and injury justification enough for giving-up the good fight, nor perhaps even the specter of death for not answering the upward call and fighting all the way to Glory."

"So how do you feel and what do you feel, and what do you feel about how you feel, and how do you feel about what you feel?"

"It just occurred to me; I wonder if Jesus
ever signed His Name."

"I am what I am, because I just pretend
I'm far better than I am …
and then I live up to it."

"I prefer daydreaming to dreaming at night,
because I have much more control over my
dreams when I'm awake."

"Yah I'm a fan of heroes,
just not everyone's."

"Too often I feel like I'm passing the baton
forward, but there's nobody up ahead
reaching back to take it."

"I have to catch myself because I'm tired of
thinking that I'm the one going crazy,
in a world that's gone bizarre."

"The only thing I don't have is what God
hasn't provided."

"In Christian parlance and in fact, God is
our Judge Jury and executioner;
Jesus the Christ—our only advocate."

"If there were no 'glamour or glory' in war,
only sadists, masochists and sociopaths
would fight them … Wait a minute!"

"SADLY, ALL I WHAT OUT OF <u>MORTAL</u> LIFE IS MORE
THAN LIFE HAS TO OFFER."

"ONLY THE DEAD NO LONGER WANT CONTROL."

"IF YOU KNOW HOW TO GET THERE,
YOU'LL KNOW WHERE YOU'RE GOING."

"IF YOU MUST BE IN THE MELEE,
YOU MIGHT AS WELL BE RIGHT IN <u>THE MIDDLE</u>
OF THE SHIT-STORM."

"I ONLY WANT SOMETHING FOR NOTHING
DEPENDING ON WHAT THE 'SOMETHING' IS
—AND THE GIVERS DEFINITION OF 'NOTHING.'"

"LET IT BE KNOWN UNEQUIVOCALLY THAT I WILL
DEFEND MYSELF WITH EXTREME PREJUDICE
AGAINST ANYONE WHO COMES AGAINST ME WITH
MALICE OF FORETHOUGHT."

"IT'S BEEN SAID THAT 'THERE'S ONLY ONE WAY TO
BEGIN AND THAT'S TO BEGIN,' FOR BEGINNING IS
NOT A PROCESS BUT AN EVENT; ONE DOESN'T
PLAN TO BEGIN, ONE BEGINS TO PLAN."

"TONGUE TWISTER THREE TIMES FAST—
'I'M GLAD I WORE MY WOOLRICH.'"

"HELL, HUBRIS FAUX-GLORY AND LIES,
IS THE STUFF THAT WAR IS MADE OF."

"HUMANITY WILL NEVER STOP UNTIL IT'S OVER."

"I'M A GREAT PROPONENT OF KEEPING BLOOD OFF
OF MY SHIRT; ESPECIALLY MY OWN."

"MAKE NO MISTAKE ABOUT IT THE ONLY RACE OF
PEOPLE GOD CARES ABOUT IS THE HUMAN RACE."

"I DEEM FAR SUPERIOR A NOBLE SAVAGE THAN A
SAVAGE NOBLE."

"HAVE WE NOT YET LEARNED FROM THE RICH AND
POWERFUL, THAT MORE IS NOT ENOUGH?"

"GOD WOULD ALWAYS HAVE US ERR ON THE SIDE
OF <u>THE SOMEONE</u> WE LOVE,
OVER <u>THE SOMETHING</u> WE LOVE."

"DON'T BE DECEIVED, FOR NOT EVERYTHING THAT
MERELY PRESENTS ITSELF IS AN OPPORTUNITY."

"WITH VERY FEW EXCEPTIONS EVERYONE'S
STRAIGHT, UNTIL THEY CHOOSE NOT TO BE."

"STRIKE WHILE THE IRON IS HOT, BECAUSE THE
SWEET-SPOT GIVEN TIME WILL ALWAYS GROW
SMALLER AS IT COOLS."

"VACATIONS ARE VERY POPULAR IN MY NEIGHBOR-
HOOD; MY NEIGHBORS ARE ALWAYS VACATING;
USUALLY BEFORE THE END OF THE MONTH AND
THE RENT'S DUE."

"TOO MANY PEOPLE THESE DAYS ALLOW THEMSELVES TO BE SO BUSY AND DISTRACTED THEY DON'T HAVE TIME FOR LIFE."

"BE PREPARED, BECAUSE MORE OFTEN THAN YOU THINK, THE ONLY WAY OF ESCAPE IS THROUGH THE 'FIRE' *YOU* STARTED."

"YOU'LL HAVE TO EXCUSE ME, BUT I CAN'T REMEMBER EVERYTHING THAT HAPPENED THE DAY I WAS BORN."

"THERE'S NEVER BEEN AN AGE IN WHICH MAN HAS NOT SHOWN HIMSELF BARBARIC."

"GOD IS CONCERNED ABOUT OUR PAIN, BUT NOT TO THE DEGREE IT MITIGATES HIS WILL."

"I DON'T DESIRE THAT ANYONE SHOULD DIE, STARTING WITH ME."

"TOO MANY PEOPLE ARE LIKE SOME CARS; TOO MUCH NOISE AND NOT MUCH POWER."

"I SAY FEEL FREE TO OVERESTIMATE YOURSELF— AND THEN MERELY LIVE-UP TO YOUR ESTIMATION."

"ONE DAY BRIGHT AND CLOUDLESS, THE DOGS OF WAR WILL BE NO MORE '…AND A LITTLE CHILD SHALL LEAD THEM.'"

"One moment in heaven with God,
or a moment in hell without Him
will be all the proof you need."

"1963 shots rang out; bells tolled;
Potus buried."

"If we were worthy of heaven, it wouldn't
be heaven now would it."

"Gray hair and whiskers grow faster than
any other hair color, because you're
growing older a whole lot quicker than
you're getting younger."

"If you're not inclined to speak the truth,
the devil will always give you the words
to say."

"Generosity makes no one poor."

"Just as a passive observer I've noticed that
dysfunction is selling these days,
because it's a buyer's market."

"There is no bravery without fear."

"Face it; not making a choice is a choice...
and rarely a good one."

"The only problem with some folks shaving
their head is that you can then see their
tectonic plates."

"VENGEANCE IS THE LORD'S AND INFINITELY PRECISE, AND WHEN HE CARRIES IT OUT, THERE IS NO UNINTENDED CONSEQUENCES, COLLATERAL DAMAGE OR INNOCENT BYSTANDERS GETTING HURT."

"SOLDERS ARE DESTROYERS THAT DESTROY OPPOSING DESTROYERS SO THAT THE BUILDERS OF THE RUINS OF THE FUTURE CAN START TO REBUILD."

"'TIS QUIXOTIC FOR … NONE OF US CAN STOP BULLETS, UNLESS <u>WE ALL OF US</u> CAN PUT DOWN THE GUN."

"I LONG FOR THE DAY WHEN PEOPLE WILL STOP DYING AND WILL FINALLY START LIVING."

"THE WORLD IS AN EXCEEDINGLY SICK PLACE, AND VERY FEW ARE SEEKING THE CURE AND WANT TO GET WELL."

"EVENTUALLY ALL MEN GET TO ASK THE QUESTION: 'WHO'S THAT OLD GUY IN THE MIRROR?'"

"I FIND THAT DISTRACTED DRIVERS ARE VERY DISTRACTING."

"A GOOD MAN KNOWS HIS LIMITATIONS, THEREFORE, I'M NOT AN ON-AIR PERSONALITY, IN FACT, I'M BARELY AN OFF-AIR PERSONALITY."

"I PERCEIVE OUR SKITTISH HUMANITY IS BEING TECHNOLOGICALLY HERDED TOWARDS 'THE FINAL ROUNDUP.'"

"I'M ALL FOR FACILITATING THE FLOW OF TRAFFIC, ESPECIALLY IN ANY VEHICLE I'M DRIVING."

"GOD DIDN'T SAY IT WAS GOING TO END WITH A WHIMPER, BUT A BANG … AND A BIG ONE!"

[A YOUNG SOLDIER'S PRAYER]
"I DON'T WANT TO KILL OR BE KILLED;
I JUST WANT TO GO HOME."

YOU'LL NEVER KNOW WHAT JOYS AWAIT
IF YOU GIVE-UP NOW."

"IF THE DISEASE IS SIN, AND WE CONTINUE SINNING, THEN WE KEEP RE-INFECTING OURSELVES."

"ALL MY LIFE I'VE BEEN A 'NOBODY;'
NOW I'M RETIRED."

"OUR EFFORT IN DOING WHAT'S RIGHT DOESN'T HAVE TO BE HEROIC OR ELEGANT …
ONLY EFFECTIVE."

"THE DEAD CARE NOTHING ABOUT WHAT THE LIVING TAKE."

"IF YOU PUT YOURSELF IN A POSITION OF WEAKNESS; EXPECT DEFEAT."

"Too many in the grand scheme of things are
nothing more than the eye-catching
annoyance of a missing pixel."

"When Satan has us on our knees, he's put
us inadvertently in the posture of prayer."

"Feel free to forsake hubris, because our
names are carved in cold granite
as soon as we're born."

"We're living in an age in which everyone is
waiting for the Xanax®
or something else to kick-in."

"No matter how many monsters in your
lifetime you defeat and destroy,
there will always be more drafted in to fill
the void."

"The God with whom we have to do is the
God of unintended turns and
consequences—
and all of them leading back to Him."

"War is hell as it ought to be, and we still
crave to fight them."

"It's easy to be strong when you're strong
it's hard to be strong when you're weak."

"The doctors do what they can,
but God does what they can't."

"The innocent always suffer as a result of sin; and the lovers of the innocent as a consequence thereof."

"The finer the cutting edge you maintain in life, the more often the need to sharpen."

"Hear ye, hear ye:
The Lord and Living God doesn't explain Himself; He declares Himself."

"I've been a human for a long time, and I know human nature, and I've studied human history, which is why I know, that by our merits, sheer will, intellect and relative morality, we're <u>none of us</u> going to make it."

"Like saying yes, being able to say no is a good quality to possess, but knowing <u>when</u> to say yes, or no, is even better."

"I'd seriously reconsider the whole thing, if your significant other insists upon rewriting the '<u>I do</u>' part of your marriage vows to include: '<u>I guess ... yah ... I don't know ... whatever</u>.'"

"Sometimes the devil doesn't bother you because he already has you where he wants you."

"Thankful to him I am, because my father's the man that made me possible."

"GUYS, THERE ARE <u>THREE THINGS</u> YOU NEVER
WANT TO BE REINCARNATED AS: A MAN WITH
PREMATURE BALDNESS, A MAN WITH IMPOTENCE
OR, <u>THE THIRD</u> MONKEY ON NOAH'S ARK."

"THE RICH FEEL THEY SHOULD HAVE WHATEVER
MONEY CAN BUY, AND THAT THEIR MONEY CAN BUY
WHATEVER THEY WANT."

"DON'T GO TO SOMEPLACE YOU DON'T NEED
TO BE TO PROCURE SOMETHING YOU DON'T NEED
TO HAVE."

"LOCKS AND BARS ON YOUR DOORS AND
WINDOWS DON'T AFFORD YOU SECURITY
AND SAFETY ... ONLY THE LUXURY OF A LITTLE
MORE TIME."

"DON'T FRET ABOUT IT, BECAUSE THE PRESENT IS
ALWAYS COMPLICATED, EVEN THE PRESENT OF
THE PAST—AND THE PRESENT IS BUT THE PAST OF
THE FUTURE."

"THE COURAGE OF TERRORISTS, TYRANTS AND
FANATICS COMES FROM THEM ALL DRINKING
THEIR OWN "KOOL-AID."

"THOSE WHO DEEM THEMSELVES UNTOUCHABLE
BY THE HAND OF PROVIDENCE
ARE DEAD MEN WALKING."

"THE ONLY CERTAINTY IN WAGING WAR IS THE
CERTAINTY OF DEATH AND THE UNCERTAINTY OF
EVERYTHING ELSE."

"LIFE ISN'T ALL ABOUT MANIPULATION, ORDERING YOUR WORLD AND ARTICULATING AND MAINTAINING PERFECTION WHILE MAKING THE UNDOABLE DOABLE AND THE UNTHINKABLE POSSIBLE, SO ... 'NO WORRIES MATE!'"

"THE WORLD'S IN THE STATE IT'S IN BECAUSE WE OF HUMANITY, NEUROTIC AND DISSATISFIED, ARE COLLECTIVELY BELIEVING OUR OWN PROPAGANDA."

"I LOOKED AT THE PICTURE ON THE SOLICITATION ENVELOPE AND WONDERED, 'HUH?' IS THIS RUGGED, GOOD-LOOKIN' BEARDED GUY REALLY HOMELESS, OR IS HE JUST AN UNEMPLOYED ACTOR POSING AND PLAYING THE PART, OR... MAYBE HE'S LEGIT, AN UNEMPLOYED ACTOR WHO'S NOW A HOMELESS GUY WITH HIS FIRST GIG." NARCISSISTS ARE PERNICIOUS AND MALIGNANT, TO WIT ... SATAN."

"ALWAYS PURSUE AND ENJOY PEACE AND QUIET, EVEN THOUGH THE QUIET OF PEACE MAY AT TIMES BE THE CALM BEFORE THE SHIT-STORM."

"LIFE ISN'T ALL ABOUT ARTICULATING PERFECTION, BUT MASTERING PEACE."

*

THE AUTHOR OF "ON THE MARK," PETER PJECHA JR., IS A CHIEF OPERATING ENGINEER [RETIRED 2016] FROM THE SCHOOL DISTRICT OF THE CITY OF ERIE PENNSYLVANIA AFTER THIRTY YEARS OF SERVICE, AND HE RESIDES IN ERIE TODAY.

PETER IS A LONG-TIME STUDENT OF PRIMITIVE CULTURES AND THEIR METHODS OF LIFE AND SURVIVAL, AS WELL AS A BEING A STUDENT OF HISTORY IN GENERAL AND A CAREFUL, KEEN OBSERVER OF HUMAN NATURE AND THE CONSEQUENCES FOR HUMANITY IN THE MODERN WORLD. THE LATTER HAS BEEN HIS SPRINGBOARD OVER THE YEARS INTO ECLECTIC, CRITICAL AND COMICAL COMMENTARY, THROUGH THE ESSENTIAL MEDIUM OF QUOTES; DIVERSE IN STYLE AND NATURE AND ADDRESSING MODERN HUMAN INTERPLAY IN A MYRIAD OF ARENAS.

HE IS ALSO AN ACCOMPLISHED CREATIVE COOK, WHO ENJOYS BOTH THE PROCESS AND THE PRODUCT; AND HE IS A LONG-TIME WINEMAKER. HE PURSUES THE DISCIPLINE OF HAIKU AND ENJOYS THE WRITING OF SHORT AND FLASH FICTION STORIES. HE ENJOYS THE THERAPEUTIC SIMPLICITY OF KNOT TYING AND JACK-KNIFE WOOD CARVING. PETER IS A CHRISTIAN STUDENT OF THE NEW AND OLD TESTAMENT OF THE BIBLE, AS WELL AS HAVING A GOOD WORKING KNOWLEDGE OF THE QURAN OF ISLAM.